NEW Close-up

B1

Alun Phillips

NATIONAL GEOGRAPHIC
LEARNING

Australia • Brazil • Canada • Mexico • Singapore • United Kingdom • United States

CREDITS

Contents

Unit 1	p 4
Unit 2	p 10
Unit 3	p 16
Unit 4	p 22
Unit 5	p 28
Unit 6	p 34
Unit 7	p 40
Unit 8	p 46
Unit 9	p 52
Unit 10	p 58
Unit 11	p 64
Unit 12	p 70
Review 1–12	**p 76**

Reading understanding the whole text; matching sentences to gaps

1 Read the Exam Reminder. Then answer the questions.

1 What is the first thing you need to do with the text?

_____

2 Which parts of the text do you need to re-read carefully?

_____

Exam REMINDER

Understanding the whole text
- Make sure you understand the general meaning, so read the whole text first.
- Read before and after the first gap: what is the specific topic?
- Read the missing sentences. Is there more than one sentence about a similar idea or topic?
- Choose the sentence that fits grammatically and logically.

2 Read and complete the Exam Task.

Exam TASK

Matching sentences to gaps

Five sentences have been removed from the text. For each question, choose the correct answer. There are three extra sentences which you do not need to use.

A The sale of the bikes gives the city extra money to spend on other services.

B There aren't many tourists around at this time, so there are fewer boats on the canals.

C He's looking for bicycles.

D However, nobody really knows why so many bikes end up in the canals.

E This is the only qualification bike fishers need.

F Unfortunately, about 15,000 of these end up in the canals every year.

G They have to do a two-week training course before starting.

H In fact, there are actually more bikes than people in Amsterdam.

Fishing for bicycles

1 We're in Amsterdam. A man is on a boat and he's looking carefully into the water. Is he looking for fish for his dinner? Not exactly. **(1)** _____ This is because he's a bike fisher. Amsterdam has got a lot of canals, around 100 kilometres in all, and also a large number of bikes – probably about a million. **(2)** _____ Whilst they're a useful way of getting around, when they end up in the canal they can be a real problem for the many boats operating in the city.

10 In the 1960s people started to fish for bikes and remove them from the canals. As a result, there are a number of official bike fishers who do the job full-time in Amsterdam. **(3)** _____ They learn a lot of things in this time, including how to look for and pick up the bikes correctly. Bike fishers can really help the environment because the metal from the bikes can be recycled and reused. The man on the boat is now pulling two dirty old bikes out of the water. He looks quite happy with himself – the bikes are in good condition. This means
20 they can be sold to a bike shop rather than go to a recycling centre. **(4)** _____

Fishing for bikes is a calm and relaxing job, just like the more traditional hobby. The bike fishers are generally busier in winter. **(5)** _____ This means the fishers have more time to search the water more carefully and find more bikes.

Vocabulary 1 jobs; personality adjectives

1 Complete the sentences with these words.

actor	architect	astronaut	athlete
camera operator	cook	firefighter	hairdresser
lawyer	librarian	politician	soldier

1 A(n) _____ is a person who performs in films and plays.
2 A(n) _____ films live events, usually for a television or cinema company.
3 A(n) _____ helps people in emergencies, especially if something is burning.
4 A(n) _____ cuts people's hair.
5 A(n) _____ prepares food for other people.
6 A(n) _____ travels in space.
7 A(n) _____ gives people advice about the law.
8 A(n) _____ has to defend his or her country in difficult situations.
9 A(n) _____ works in a place with lots of books and other media that people can use or borrow.
10 A(n) _____ helps to manage the country.
11 A(n) _____ is usually very fit and trains for competitions.
12 A(n) _____ designs new buildings.

2 Choose one of these adjectives to describe each person.

cheerful	confident	lazy	patient
shy	sociable		

1 Talia never does any homework. She's so _____ .
2 My brother is very _____ and never talks to anyone that he doesn't know.
3 My history teacher is very _____ and doesn't get angry if you make a mistake.
4 I was a bit nervous during my first few driving lessons, but now I feel much more _____ .
5 Everybody looks _____ when the weather is good. They're all smiling and happy.
6 My flatmate is very _____ and often meets up with friends.

3 Complete the description with these words.

anxious	cheerful	confident	generous
hard-working	honest	nervous	patient
reliable	shy		

My cousin Michelle is a very [1] _____ person and she worries a lot about things in general. She's really [2] _____ before big exams, for example. Luckily, she's a very [3] _____ student and she always gets good results because she studies so much. She was quite [4] _____ and didn't speak much when she was younger, especially to people she didn't know. Now she speaks much more and looks quite [5] _____ when she's with others.

In general, she's not a very [6] _____ person and doesn't smile or laugh much. But I like her because she's [7] _____ and is always on time. She's also very [8] _____ and never says things that aren't true. She's quite [9] _____ and always lends me her clothes when I want to borrow them. I also think she's very [10] _____ because she stops and listens when you want to explain or talk about something.

4 Choose the correct option to complete the sentences.

1 She's always helping other people. She's a very *generous / serious* person.
2 My aunt works ten hours a day and at weekends. She's very *confident / hard-working*.
3 Jules never worries about anything. He's so *relaxed / nervous*.
4 He never gets up before 10 a.m. and doesn't work hard. I think he's really *lazy / unkind*.
5 It's cold and wet, and everybody on the bus looks *miserable / cheerful*.
6 Some of his friends were very *sociable / jealous* of his success.
7 Greta always does what she promises. She's very *anxious / reliable*.
8 She's very *confident / hard-working* in all kinds of social situations.
9 Those people were very *unkind / lazy* to you just now.
10 My friend is very *unkind / patient* and always waits for me when I'm late.
11 I have a test tomorrow, but I feel really *calm / shy* about it because I have studied a lot.
12 Driving fast in the city centre is really *patient / dangerous*.

Grammar 1 present simple and present continuous; stative verbs

1 Complete the sentences with the present simple or present continuous.

   1 I _____ (take) the early train on Wednesdays and Fridays.

   2 Lin often _____ (help) the staff in a local café.

   3 These machines _____ (work) very well when it's cold.

   4 We _____ (have) three hours of lessons on Monday mornings.

   5 Can we speak later? I _____ (watch) a film.

   6 What time _____ (you / leave) for school tomorrow?

2 Choose the correct option to complete the sentences.

   1 My sister *owns / is owning* a shop.

   2 *I'm seeing / I see* a few friends later.

   3 My little brother *is / is being* very shy.

   4 *I don't like / I'm not liking* Indian food.

   5 This sandwich *is tasting / tastes* really good.

   6 *We're meeting / We meet* just after dinner this evening.

3 Complete the text with the present simple or present continuous form of the verb in brackets.

People say that my sister and I ¹_____ (be) similar, but I ²_____ (not believe) that. She's a firefighter. She ³_____ (work) hard, often in difficult situations. At the moment, she ⁴_____ (do) a special training course at a fire station in London.

My sister ⁵_____ (say) that fires often ⁶_____ (start) because people ⁷_____ (not think) about the possible dangers in their homes. She ⁸_____ (always / tell) me to turn off my computer and TV.

Listening choosing the correct picture; multiple choice with picture options

1 Read the Exam Reminder. What do you need to do before listening?

_____

2 **1.1 ▶** Listen and complete the Exam Task.

Exam TASK

Multiple choice with picture options

For each question, choose the correct answer.

   1 What job does Alice's uncle do?

      A   B   C

   2 What time do they decide to watch the film?

      A   B   C

   3 How does Carrie's brother feel today?

      A   B   C

   4 What job does Maria do?

      A   B   C

   5 Where does Marcel work?

      A   B   C

▶ **Grammar references 1.1 and 1.2, p161 in Student's Book**

Vocabulary 2 employment vocabulary; life events

1 Match the words (1–6) with the definitions (a–f).

1 candidate ☐
2 full-time ☐
3 part-time ☐
4 qualification ☐
5 retired ☐
6 unemployed ☐

a If you pass an exam at school or university, or finish a course, you get this.
b when you work the maximum number of hours in your job
c when you haven't got a job
d someone who is applying for a job
e when you work less than the maximum number of hours in a week
f when you aren't working anymore because you have reached a certain age

2 Complete the sentences with the words (1–6) from Exercise 1.

1 This person is an interesting _____ for the new job.
2 I used to work _____ , 35 hours a week or more, but now I work _____ and only do twenty hours a week.
3 My mum worked as a teacher for forty-five years, but now she's nearly 70 and is _____ .
4 My cousin had a few jobs, but at the moment he's _____ and can't find work.
5 I really want to apply for that job, but I don't think I've got the right _____ .

3 Choose the correct words to complete the sentences.

1 My cousin *got / did* married last year.
2 My friend is a cook, but he's *out / off* of work at the moment.
3 His parents died when he was four, so he was *grown up / brought up* by his grandparents.
4 My uncle *brought up / grew up* in a small village in Ireland.
5 My friend *split up with / applied for* her boyfriend last week.
6 My sister is going out *with / to* one of my classmates.
7 I really hope to go *at / to* college next year.
8 I've applied *for / on* hundreds of jobs, but can't find one.

4 Complete the sentences with the correct form of these words or expressions.

apply for	be brought up	candidates
get married	go out with	go to university
grow up	out of work	retired
split up with		

My dad was born in Italy, but [1] _____ in La Rochelle in France because his family moved there when he was very young. His mum and dad worked really hard, so he [2] _____ by his grandmother. He started work at sixteen, so he didn't [3] _____ to study. He [4] _____ a girl at school for a few years, but he decided to [5] _____ her when he went to look for work in Paris. He was [6] _____ for the first six months, but then he [7] _____ a job as a camera operator on French TV. There were more than a hundred [8] _____ for the job, but Dad got it! He met my mum at work a few weeks later and they [9] _____ just two months after that. He worked in film studios for over 40 years, but now he's [10] _____ and enjoys being a grandfather.

Grammar 2 countable and uncountable nouns; quantifiers

1 **Write these words in the correct column.**

advice   candidate   coffee   dinner
family   friend   hair   information   milk
news   person   qualification   tea

Countable	Uncountable	Both (depending on context)

2 **Complete the sentences with these words. Use an article (a, an) if necessary.**

advice   architect   break   hockey
information   milk   friend   qualification

1 I'm trying to find _____ about the new opening times.
2 I have _____ who goes to your school.
3 Do you play _____ in a local team?
4 Is your mum _____ ?
5 I need your _____ about my future career.
6 Shall we take _____ now?
7 I have _____ in engineering.
8 I don't want _____ in my coffee, thanks.

3 **Complete the sentences with the correct present simple form of the verb be.**

1 Where _____ the information I am looking for?
2 There _____ a lot of people in my family.
3 That _____ great advice. Thanks, Dad!
4 Maths _____ my favourite subject at school.
5 Their children _____ always so cheerful.
6 The food _____ good in this restaurant.
7 There _____ snow on the ground.
8 The news _____ not good, I'm afraid.
9 The chocolate _____ in the kitchen.
10 The chocolates _____ delicious.

4 **Choose the correct option to complete the sentences.**

1 I've got a little / a few chocolate if you're hungry.
2 Can I give you an / some advice?
3 I think we'll need a kilo / a little of bananas as well.
4 This is a / some delicious cake.
5 I'd like to watch a few / a little films on TV this weekend.
6 We haven't got any / some people working part-time at the moment.
7 Would you like some / much coffee?
8 How many / much milk would you like?

5 **Complete the sentences with these words and phrases.**

a kilo   lot of   a number   a few   a little
many   much

1 Would you like _____ cheese?
2 Can I speak to you for _____ minutes?
3 How _____ yoghurt do we need for the cake?
4 Can you buy _____ of tomatoes, please?
5 It's summer and there are a _____ tourists in town.
6 How _____ people did you invite?
7 There are _____ of good cafés around here.

6 **Complete the text with these words and phrases.**

a lot   any   few   little   many   much
number of   some

Most people think actors earn ¹_____
of money and have very ²_____
work to do all day. Well, that's true for
³_____ well-known actors and a
small ⁴_____ them can earn millions
of dollars for just one film. In fact, there are actors
who haven't got very ⁵_____ work
and others who are unemployed and haven't
got ⁶_____ work at all. Also, there
aren't usually ⁷_____ good acting jobs,
so some actors have to take a ⁸_____
other jobs, just to pay the bills.

Grammar references 1.3 and 1.4, p162 in Student's Book

Writing using informal language; including all the information; writing an email

1 **Match the informal sentences (1–6) with the more formal ones (a–f).**

1 Fantastic news! _____

2 Sorry, can't come Saturday. _____

3 Hi Freida _____

4 See you in the morning. _____

5 Awesome film! _____

6 Best wishes _____

a Dear Ms Horton

b That is really good news.

c I am sorry, but I cannot attend on Saturday.

d I think the film was really good.

e I look forward to seeing you at 10 a.m. tomorrow.

f Yours sincerely

2 **Rewrite these sentences so they are less formal.**

1 I look forward to seeing you this evening.

_____

2 That is really bad news.

_____

3 I am sorry, but I will not be present at your party.

_____

4 I would really like to meet your friends.

_____

5 I think the restaurant is really good.

_____

3 **Read the Exam Reminder. How many different points do you need to include in your answer?**

_____

4 **Read Yvonne's email and Luke's reply. Has Luke covered all four points?**

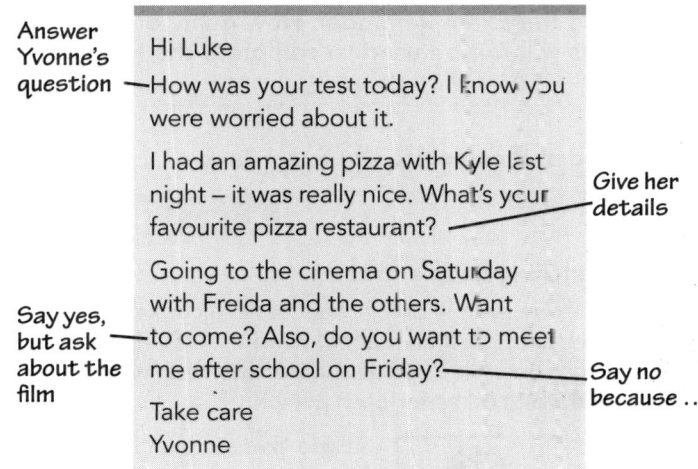

Answer Yvonne's question

Hi Luke

How was your test today? I know you were worried about it.

I had an amazing pizza with Kyle last night – it was really nice. What's your favourite pizza restaurant? — Give her details

Going to the cinema on Saturday with Freida and the others. Want to come? Also, do you want to meet me after school on Friday? — Say no because ...

Say yes, but ask about the film

Take care
Yvonne

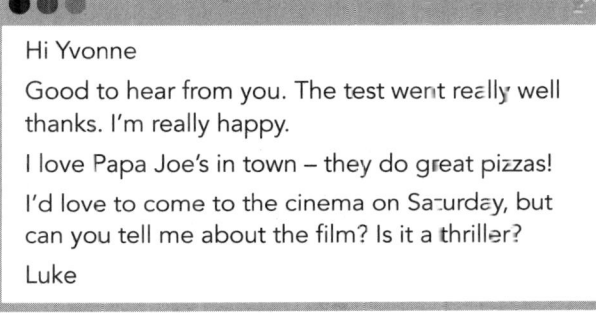

Hi Yvonne

Good to hear from you. The test went really well thanks. I'm really happy.

I love Papa Joe's in town – they do great pizzas!

I'd love to come to the cinema on Saturday, but can you tell me about the film? Is it a thriller?

Luke

5 **Read and complete the Exam Task. Don't forget to use the Useful Language on page 15 of your Student's Book.**

Exam TASK

Writing an email

Read this email from your English-speaking friend Viktor and the notes you have made.

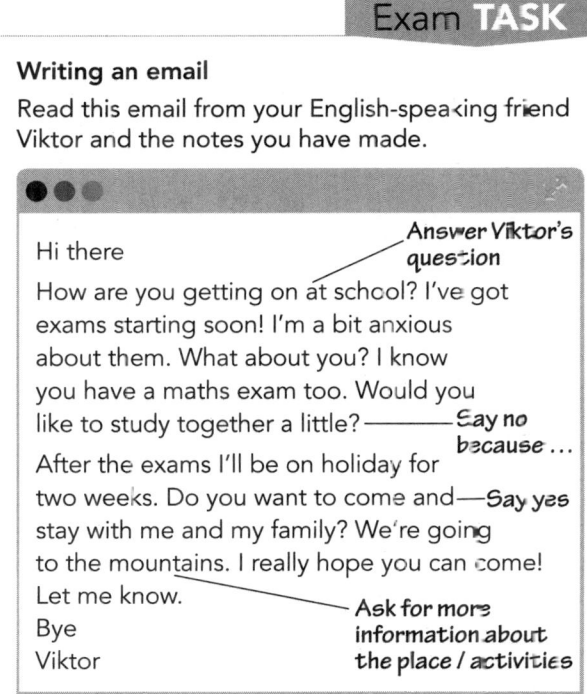

Hi there

How are you getting on at school? I've got exams starting soon! I'm a bit anxious about them. What about you? I know you have a maths exam too. Would you like to study together a little? — Say no because ...

Answer Viktor's question

After the exams I'll be on holiday for two weeks. Do you want to come and — Say yes stay with me and my family? We're going to the mountains. I really hope you can come! Let me know. — Ask for more information about the place / activities

Bye
Viktor

Write a reply to Viktor in about **100 words**.

Reading reading for detail; matching people to texts

1 Read the Exam Reminder. How many of the eight texts will *not* be used to complete the task?

_____

2 Read and complete the Exam Task.

Exam TASK

Matching people to texts

The five people below want to do a cooking course in another country. Read the descriptions of eight possible courses and decide which would be the best course for each person.

1  Sabine likes simple food. She doesn't like fish or vegetables much, but loves meat and wants to barbecue for friends at weekends. _____

2  Kiren often cooks for family and friends. He wants to stay in a city and learn traditional home cooking. He's only got a few days free to do a course. _____

3  Gina loves nature and quiet places. She's really keen on desserts and wants to go somewhere with her two boys, aged 8 and 10. _____

4  Alessia wants to see new places, especially outside Europe, and learn about other cultures. She prefers cooking vegetables to meat, but doesn't like spicy food or cakes. _____

5  Youssef hasn't got any cooking experience. He loves simple, inexpensive food. He loves trying original food. He also likes spending his free time by the sea. _____

Exam REMINDER

Reading for detail

• You need to match five people to the text that fits the person best from eight choices.

• Start by reading about the five people. Underline the key points for each person.

• Read all the texts. Take one text and see if the text matches ALL the key points that you underlined for the first person. If not, go to the next text and see if it matches all the points for that person.

• Go back and check all your answers again.

A Cook dinner with Nonna

1 Have you ever wanted to cook like Grandma? This is a three-day course for experienced cooks who want to learn real Italian cooking in the heart of Rome. Two local grandmothers, Nonna Bruna and Nonna Antonella will show you how to cook a full Italian meal. From starters to your own pasta, delicious Roman meat dishes and homemade desserts, the grandmothers have all the answers.

B Lebanese cooking class with a local family

This is a great experience especially if you want to
10 try great food and learn the local way of life. You will stay and eat with Tania and her family in Beirut for two weeks. She'll show you how to make dishes like hummus, soups, beans and rice, baked chicken with potatoes as well as traditional snacks.

C Silom Thai Cooking School in Bangkok

Here, you can learn how to make tasty Thai dishes. We use a lot of hot spices in our food and you can make great fried rice dishes with meat and fish. We will also teach you to prepare sweet and sour vegetable dishes and our famous Thai green curry.

D Baking and pastry classes on a Swedish farm

20 Sweden is famous for its cakes and here, in a small Swedish village, you can learn how to bake them. This course is great for people with young children. They can play or help on the farm while you learn to make a sweet tiger cake for them for afternoon tea.

E Traditional cooking course in Buenos Aires

Juan and Marina will show you how to cook beef and lamb the traditional Argentinian way. Here we like to keep things simple, so no spices or sauces. But we'll teach you how to grill the right way and how to make a real wood fire.

Vocabulary 1
taste; cooking verbs; choosing the correct option; multiple-choice cloze

1 Choose the correct option to complete the sentences.

1 I love *salty / sweet* snacks, but my best friend prefers chocolate and cakes.
2 This yoghurt is a bit too *sour / spicy* for me.
3 I like *bitter / spicy* food and often put hot peppers on my pasta.
4 These grapes are so *sour / sweet*. They're lovely.
5 Please could you put some more sugar in this lemonade as it's too *bitter / sweet*.

2 Complete the sentences with these words.

bake	barbecue	boil	fry	grill	roast

1 You need to _____ this cake in the oven for about 30 minutes.
2 First _____ some water and then put the pasta in.
3 Let's _____ everything outside.
4 Please _____ the eggs in a little oil.
5 I like to _____ fish rather than fry it. It's a healthier way to cook it.
6 I love it when we _____ a chicken in the oven for a family lunch.

F Language and lunch in Montpellier

30 This course teaches you two things at the same time – you learn modern French cooking and how to speak French. Your chef will explain how to prepare delicious French dishes such as roasted chicken and vegetables. You can then eat and discuss the dishes with other students. The course is suitable for people with some experience of cooking.

G Katerina's Kouzina

You love tasty Greek food. You want to learn how to make it yourself, but you've never cooked before. No problem. Stay on the Greek island of Poros for two
40 weeks and Katerina will teach you how to bake, roast and grill in the traditional way. She will also show you how to make modern, creative Greek dishes using local meat and freshly caught fish.

H Abbey Home Farm, England: Natural Kitchen cookery course

The course is perfect for vegetarians. We start by showing you how to make healthy green smoothies. Our top chef then teaches you how to make homemade bread, delicious salty snacks and an amazing bitter lemon cake. She will show you that natural dishes and ingredients are good for you and
50 your family.

---

3 Read the Exam Reminder and complete the Exam Task.

Exam REMINDER

Choosing the correct option
- You need to complete the gaps in a short text.
- Read the whole text before you begin.
- Look at each gap in turn. Read the text just before and after it.
- Think about a possible word to put in the gap.
- If it's a verb, think of the correct form. For example, do I need the past with -ed, or do I need the -ing form?
- Look at the four options and find the best word for the gap.
- Read the text again and check that all your answers make sense.

Exam TASK

Multiple-choice cloze
For each question, choose the correct answer.

In Britain, National Fish and Chip Day is on 2nd June. But where does this popular ¹ _____ actually come from? Chips aren't a British invention after all. People started to ² _____ potatoes in Belgium and France long before they did in Britain. They ³ _____ them when it was impossible to catch fish because of frozen lakes and rivers. Fried fish isn't a British invention either. It actually came from Spanish and Portuguese people living in the UK who didn't like the ⁴ _____ fish they were offered.

It was a businessman called John Lees who first started to serve fish and chips ⁵ _____ in 1863.

Fish and chips are still a ⁶ _____ choice in England. In fact, there are more than 10,500 fish and chip shops across the country.

1 A dish	B plate	C eat	D eating
2 A make	B fry	C barbecuing	D cooking
3 A saw	B making	C do	D ate
4 A sour	B boiled	C barbecue	D sweet
5 A together	B all	C between	D either
6 A taste	B likely	C popular	D really

Grammar 1 past simple; past continuous

1 **Complete the sentences with the past simple form of these verbs.**

find	give	lose	spend	start	take

1 We _____ a nice restaurant in the square.

2 I _____ the early train yesterday.

3 Dad _____ us €10 for some food.

4 Ana _____ a new yoga course last week.

5 My friends and I _____ the morning watching TV.

6 We _____ 0–6 in last Friday's match. It was terrible!

2 **Complete the sentences with the past continuous form of these verbs.**

cook	drive	have	read	shop
snow	watch			

1 I didn't answer the phone because I _____ a film.

2 I _____ a shower at six thirty this morning.

3 I _____ the fish while Karl _____ the recipe.

4 It was a cold day and it _____ outside.

5 I _____ to the cinema when you called me.

6 It was a Saturday afternoon and lots of people _____ in town.

3 **Complete the text with the past simple or past continuous form of the verb in brackets.**

It was July and I ¹_____ (work) in a restaurant for the summer. One day, I ²_____ (help) the chef in the kitchen. He ³_____ (fry) fish when his phone ⁴_____ (ring). He ⁵_____ (go) outside and ⁶_____ (forget) about the food he ⁷_____ (cook). Soon, smoke ⁸_____ (come) out of the kitchen. When the chef ⁹_____ (come) back in, lots of people ¹⁰_____ (try) to stop the fire. The chef ¹¹_____ (apologise) to everybody, but his boss ¹²_____ (not be) happy with him.

Listening identifying the key words; multiple choice with one conversation

1 **Read the Exam Reminder. What do you need to find in the questions and the options?**

_____

2 **2.1 ▶ Listen and complete the Exam Task.**

Exam TASK

Multiple choice with one conversation

For each question, choose the correct answer. You will hear a podcast about a famous food destination.

1 Santiago is
   A a mix of different cultures.
   B in the mountains.
   C by the sea.

2 In the Central Market in Santiago, the best thing to do is
   A make your own sandwich.
   B buy fruit and vegetables.
   C eat in one of the restaurants inside the market.

3 La Vega market is
   A a fish market.
   B open every day.
   C an open-air market.

4 The Bellavista area
   A doesn't have large apartments or office blocks.
   B is busier during the day than at night.
   C has lots of international restaurants.

5 The Peumayén restaurant
   A always has the same menu.
   B serves traditional Chilean food.
   C is busiest in the early evening.

6 The poet Pablo Neruda
   A owned a local restaurant.
   B created a menu for one restaurant.
   C writes about Bellavista restaurants in his work.

↻ Grammar references 2.1 and 2.2, p163 in Student's Book

Vocabulary 2 tableware; packaging and quantities

1 Complete the labels with these words.

bunch	glass	packet	piece	slice	tin

1 a _____ of bananas

2 a _____ of juice

3 a _____ of beans

4 a _____ of bread

5 a _____ of cheese

6 a _____ of crisps

2 Match the packaging on the left (1–5) with a word on the right (a–e).

1 a slice / piece of ☐   a soup
2 a packet of ☐   b cake
3 a tin of ☐   c biscuits
4 a bunch of ☐   d water
5 a jug of ☐   e grapes

3 Choose the correct option to complete the sentences.

1 Can you buy me a *bunch / tin* of tuna, please?
2 We ordered two *jugs / bowls* of orange juice for breakfast.
3 I normally have two *cups / jars* of coffee before I go to work.
4 I bought a *box / bowl* of those snacks you like.
5 My grandma makes delicious jam – would you like a *jug / jar*?
6 Please pass me the bread *knife / fork* so I can cut a slice for you.
7 I always start the day with a *bowl / cup* of cereal.
8 Can I have a clean *tin / plate* for my sandwich?

4 Complete the sentences with these words.

bowl	box	cups	fork	jars	jug
knife	plates	saucers			

1 We've got lots of cups but no _____ to go with them.
2 I drank three _____ of tea this morning.
3 Shall we buy Grandpa a _____ of chocolates for his birthday?
4 Can you get me a clean _____ for the salad?
5 I think there are a few _____ of honey in the cupboard.
6 In some places, people don't eat with a _____ and _____ . They eat with their hands.
7 We need some big _____ for the pizza.
8 Let's ask for a _____ of water to have with the meal.

5 Complete the text with these words.

bottles	bowl (x2)	cup	glass	jar
packets	slices			

I work in a large factory near my home. My working day starts at 6 a.m. with a small [1] _____ of yoghurt and fresh fruit and a [2] _____ of coffee. Sometimes, I also have a couple of [3] _____ of toast. It's really hot where I work, so I take lots of [4] _____ of water with me. I also keep a few [5] _____ of biscuits in a cupboard because I get hungry around 10 o'clock.

We stop at midday for about half an hour and I have a [6] _____ of soup or a salad in the canteen with my colleagues. After work, we sometimes go for a quick snack in town, but I normally just have a [7] _____ of orange juice. When I get home, I'll have something quick and easy for dinner – maybe some fish and rice. I'll often eat some olives straight from the [8] _____ while I'm waiting for the fish to cook. I love olives. They're delicious! Then I sit down to watch a good film while I'm eating.

Grammar 2 *used to* and *would*; *be used to* and *get used to*

1 Choose the correct option to complete the sentences.

1 She *used to / would* live next door to me.

2 We *wouldn't / didn't use to* enjoy our maths lessons, but now they're fun.

3 *Did you use to / Would you* be afraid of the dark when you were younger?

4 My younger brother *used eating / used to eat* a lot of biscuits, but now he prefers fruit.

5 We *would often stay / use often stay* with our grandparents during the summer holidays.

6 I *didn't use to be / wouldn't be* so tired in the mornings.

7 *Would your parents / Used your parents to* listen to programmes on the radio a lot?

8 My mum *would / used to* know all my friends, but now she never meets any of them.

2 Complete the sentences with the correct form of *used to* or *would* and these words.

grow	have	help	live	not/watch	wait

1 My brother _____ me with my homework in my first year at secondary school.

2 We _____ outside the cinema for hours to go and see the latest film.

3 We _____ a cat and a dog, but now we've only got the cat.

4 Where _____ your parents _____ ?

5 My friends _____ that TV show, but now they do.

6 My grandma _____ her own vegetables, but now she buys them.

3 Choose the correct option to complete the sentences.

1 Did it take a long time to *be used to / get used to* your new job?

2 *I'm not used to / I don't get used to* the hot weather here.

3 Did your brother *use to / get used to* living in a big city?

4 I don't think my grandparents ever *got used to / were used to* their new home out of town.

5 *They didn't get used to / They didn't used to* waking up so early.

6 When I first arrived, I *didn't get used / wasn't used to* all the noise from the street.

7 I *can't get used to / can't be used to* speaking a foreign language all day.

8 We *aren't used / didn't use* to having so much homework.

4 Complete the sentences with the correct form of *be used to* and *get used to*.

1 It wasn't easy at first, but now I _____ to working with my new colleagues.

2 I _____ the traffic because I've lived here all my life.

3 I couldn't _____ Thai food when I first moved there.

4 _____ you _____ your new class teacher now?

5 Was it difficult to _____ speaking a new language?

6 At the beginning, we _____ people's accents, but now we speak just like them.

7 I _____ all the rain we get. I prefer sunshine.

8 It took her a long time to _____ all the attention she got as a sports star.

5 Complete the conversations with one word in each gap.

1 A: I have to get _____ to my new diet. What about you?

   B: Oh, no problems. I _____ used to it now.

2 A: Did you _____ to drink coffee when you were younger?

   B: No, I _____ not!

3 A: We _____ always go fishing on Sundays when I was young.

   B: Really? We didn't use _____ do anything.

4 A: How's the new job? Are you _____ to working at night now?

   B: Well, I'm _____ used to it, I suppose.

➔ Grammar references 2.3 and 2.4, p163 in Student's Book

Writing
using adjectives and adverbs; planning and organisation; writing an article

1 Circle the word that doesn't belong in each group.

1 place: fried traditional modern clean
2 food: tasty rude dull burnt
3 service: rude unfriendly raw fast
4 food: delicious dull tasty dirty
5 origin: Greek unhealthy Indian Spanish
6 food: colourful salty friendly bitter

2 Write the adjectives in the correct order.

1 We ate a(n) _____ pizza. (Italian / big / round)

2 My uncle has a(n) _____ car. (old / fantastic / black)

3 My friend bought a _____ cake at the shop. (chocolate / tasty / little)

4 It's a(n) _____ restaurant. (French / old-fashioned / clean)

5 I've got a(n) _____ painting on my wall. (Indian / wonderful / modern)

6 I found a _____ object on the floor. (metal / round / colourful)

3 Read the Exam Reminder. What's the first thing you need to do when you write your article?

_____

4 Read the writing task. Then read the student's plan.

You see this on a friend's English language blog.

What are the two most popular local restaurants?

Why are they popular?

What's your opinion of them?

Write your answer in about **100 words**.

Student's plan:

Paragraph 1

Top Tacos – Mexican

Empress – Indian

Paragraph 2

Top Tacos – new, modern, spicy

Empress – bright, colourful place, tasty food, cheap

Paragraph 3

Top Tacos: portions good, very hot and spicy food, lots of people, slow service

Empress: friendly staff, delicious food

5 Now read the student's article. Are all the points in the plan in the final article?

_____

There are two popular restaurants in my local town: Top Tacos, a Mexican restaurant, and The Empress, an Indian restaurant.

People like Top Tacos because it's bright and modern inside and it's a great place for spicy food, but is a bit crowded on busy evenings. The Empress is a bright and modern restaurant too. I think it's so popular because the food is really tasty, but it's a so very cheap.

I tried both restaurants. I liked the food in Top Tacos because the portions were really good, but the food was too spicy for me. I wouldn't recommend it because of the large number of people in the place. The service was so slow!

6 Read and complete the Exam Task. Don't forget to use the Useful Language on page 27 of your Student's Book.

Exam TASK

Writing an article

You see this notice on a website you like:

Hi everyone!

We want to hear about a bad eating out experience you had.

Tell us about the restaurant:

- Say why it was so bad
- Explain your opinion

Write your answer in about **100 words**.

Reading
reading for general understanding; multiple choice with one text

1 Read the Exam Reminder. What do you need to find the first time you read?

An arctic wolf spider

Warmer Earth:
BIGGER spiders

1 The Arctic is well-known for its ice and glaciers. The area also contains a variety of different ecosystems with complex food webs. You might think it is extremely difficult for any animal to stay alive in temperatures of up to -50°C in the winter months, but many do thanks to their special adaptations to deal with extreme conditions.

Greenhouse gases – gases that stop heat from escaping out of the Earth's atmosphere – have played a large part in warming the planet for the last few decades.
10 Greenhouse gases are released through some human activities such as driving cars, but they are also released through natural processes like decomposition. Because the Arctic is so cold for much of the year, decomposition happens slowly there, and thus there is a large build-up of this decaying matter in the ground. In fact, across much of the Arctic, the ground is permanently frozen as 'permafrost'. This permafrost begins to thaw when temperatures become warmer, which is happening now. This means that there is more decaying matter that can
20 now be decomposed by fungus and bacteria. Through this increased decomposition, even more greenhouse gases are released to the atmosphere, which of course makes climate change happen even faster.

Like in most places, spiders are common predators in arctic ecosystems. Although spiders resemble insects in some ways, they actually belong to a group of animals called 'arachnids'. Amanda Koltz, an arctic ecologist at Washington University in St. Louis, has been studying one common type of arctic spider, the wolf spider, and
30 how it deals with a changing climate. Koltz's main goal is to understand how animals like wolf spiders respond to increasing temperatures in the Arctic and in turn, what the consequences are for the food web and ecosystem.

The wolf spider is important in the region because it is one of the top predators in many areas, at least among the smaller animals. Wolf spiders eat a lot of *springtails*, which are tiny animals that feed on the fungus responsible for decomposition. Koltz and others have also found out that as the Arctic warms,
40 wolf spiders are becoming bigger and reproducing more because they have more time to eat during the summer! This suggests that there might be more wolf spiders in the Arctic as the region becomes warmer and warmer. More spiders also might mean that they eat more springtails. Fewer springtails could lead to more uneaten fungus and more decomposition, thereby increasing the release of greenhouse gases from arctic soils. However, to her surprise, quite the opposite happens.

50 In warmer conditions, and when they found themselves in a crowd, the spiders actually ate less than usual. Koltz does not know the reason for this yet but she thinks it could be that the combination of the crowding and warmer temperatures makes spiders change their eating habits. In fact, it appears as though the spiders tend to eat each other and other spiders more often when they are crowded. The result of this change in feeding habits is that when it is warm and when there are more spiders, more springtail prey are left uneaten. The springtail prey
60 are then left to eat a lot of the fungus, which leads to less decomposition happening. Having more spiders could actually mean that fewer greenhouse gases are released to the atmosphere!

Although larger animals receive a lot of attention in the Arctic and elsewhere, Koltz wants to change this. As she has shown in the case of wolf spiders, even tiny animals can have important effects on ecosystems.

2 Read and complete the Exam Task.

Multiple choice with one text

For each question, choose the correct answer.

1 We learn from the article that

   A there are hardly any animals in the Arctic region.

   B it is too cold in the winter for most animals to survive in the Arctic.

   C climate change is also affecting the Arctic region.

   D the winters in the Arctic are getting colder.

2 'Permafrost'

   A creates greenhouse gases.

   B is a type of fungus.

   C is decreasing in the Arctic region.

   D is dangerous for the soil.

3 According to the article, Amanda Koltz

   A believes most people do not know that spiders are animals.

   B is an expert in studying different kinds of spiders.

   C is investigating the reason behind climate change.

   D wants to know why there are fewer springtails in the Arctic.

4 The article says that wolf spiders

   A are growing in number because of climate change.

   B are harmful for the environment.

   C only eat springtails.

   D are dying because of hotter temperatures.

5 The main thing that Koltz discovered from her research was that

   A wolf spiders eat more when there are a lot of other spiders around.

   B wolf spiders' size and eating habits are changing.

   C wolf spiders are eating each other more often than in the past.

   D large animals receive more attention than small ones like spiders.

Two springtails eating fungus

Vocabulary 1 geographical features climate change

1 Choose the correct option to complete the sentences.

1 This is a beautiful green *stream / valley* with just a few houses and lovely fields.

2 The temperature is hotter so the *glacier / cliff* is much smaller this year.

3 I'd like to visit a real *coast / rainforest* because I love trees, plants and insects.

4 When the weather is good, you can see the *coast / ocean* of that island really clearly.

5 I like exploring *streams / caves*, but I'm a bit scared of the bats that live there.

6 Stay away from the edge of the *cliff / valley*.

7 The children love playing in water. Luckily, we have a small *stream / ocean* near our house.

8 I love watching the boats on the *valley / ocean*.

2 Complete the sentences with these phrases.

| climate change | fossil fuels | power station |
| renewable energy | solar power | |

1 Energy that comes from the sun is called
_____ .

2 Common types of _____ include gas and oil.

3 Using the wind to create electricity is an example of _____ .

4 The most obvious example of _____ is higher temperatures.

5 The people around here don't want them to build a new _____ .

3 Complete the text using the phrases from Exercise 2.

I think our future depends on using more
[1]_____ such as wind and
[2]_____ . We need to use fewer
[3]_____ because they create a lot of pollution. In the future, we will still need a
[4]_____ to provide energy for the local population, but it's also important to remember the problem of [5]_____ when we build new ones.

Grammar 1 present perfect simple; present perfect continuous

1 Complete the sentences with the present perfect simple of these verbs.

change	just/eat	just/finish	leave
win	work		

1 I _____ my last exam and now I can relax for a few weeks.
2 My brother's a doctor and he _____ in several big hospitals.
3 I _____ a delicious meal at that new restaurant.
4 Our coach is really pleased because we _____ every match so far this season.
5 The climate _____ in the last twenty years.
6 I think I _____ my phone at home.

2 Complete the sentences with the present perfect continuous of these verbs.

get	look	study	not train	travel	wait

1 Our summers _____ warmer over the last few years.
2 He _____ much recently and his football coach isn't happy.
3 Jeff and Ana _____ all around Asia since January.
4 You _____ a lot recently. Have you got exams soon?
5 Sorry I'm late. _____ you _____ long?
6 Oh, there you are. I _____ for you everywhere.

3 Complete the sentences with the present perfect simple or present perfect continuous of the verbs in brackets.

1 They want to build ten new power stations, but so far they _____ (complete) only one.
2 I _____ (not / see) you for a long time. What _____ (you / do) recently?
3 That company _____ (spend) over £1bn on clean energy.
4 I _____ (not meet) Tania yet.
5 _____ (you / see) my keys anywhere?
6 I _____ (try) to contact you all morning.

Listening predicting the type of answer needed; gap fill

1 Read the Exam Reminder. Apart from words, what else might you need to write in the gaps?

_____

2 **3.1** ▶ Listen and complete the Exam Task.

Exam TASK

Gap fill

You will hear a programme about Norway and what it is doing about climate change.

For each question, write the correct answer in the gap. Write one, two or three words, or a number or a date or a time.

1 Norway has used its rivers to produce energy for more than _____ years.
2 Norway now gets _____ of its electricity from water.
3 The rest of its energy comes from solar energy and _____ .
4 Norway had 50,000 electric cars on its roads in _____ .
5 Every year, about _____ people buy a new electric car.
6 Norway produces lots of _____ and it sells these to Europe.

↻ Grammar references 3.1 and 3.2, p163–164 in Student's Book

Vocabulary 2 environment verbs; prepositions (1)

1 Choose the correct word to complete the sentences.

1 We *reached / collected* the station ten minutes before the train left.

2 There was a terrible storm and it *destroyed / prevented* a lot of houses.

3 The doctor's quick action *set up / prevented* a disaster.

4 There was an accident, but everybody *destroyed / survived*.

5 We *set up / reached* an online group to discuss environmental problems.

6 My favourite mug fell on the floor and it *destroyed / broke* into lots of pieces.

7 There was a parcel for me at the post office, so I went to *reach / collect* it.

8 We were able to *prevent / remove* a lot of rubbish from our local river.

2 Complete the text with the correct form of the verbs in Exercise 1.

After finding out about people who have changed the world during a lesson at school one day, two teenage sisters from Bali decided to make a difference. Melati and Isabel Wijsen ¹_____ the Bye Bye Plastic Bags group. A lot of single-use plastic bags pollute the sea around Bali. Fish eat these plastic bags. When the bags ²_____ their stomachs, the fish become ill. Many do not ³_____. The bags also ⁴_____ into little pieces in the water and cause serious problems for other marine life which think they are food and try to eat them.

The sisters have created several recycling projects to ⁵_____ as many plastic bags as possible before they end up in the sea. They go to local towns and schools and teach people that plastic bags can ⁶_____ the local marine life that many people depend on. They give people non-plastic bags to use and also show them simple ways to ⁷_____ plastic bags from ending up in the water in their local rivers. They also teach them how to ⁸_____ bags that are already in the water.

3 Complete the sentences with these prepositions.

at	before	from	in	into	over
onto	to				

1 We use many types of renewable energy, _____ wind power to solar energy.

2 There are very few recycling places _____ our town.

3 They turned the old power station _____ a modern recycling centre.

4 We've been going _____ the same summer concert for more than ten years.

5 We've been waiting for you for _____ twenty minutes.

6 We're studying wind power at school _____ present.

7 Make sure that none of that paint gets _____ your clothes.

8 Not many people drove electric cars _____ 2015.

4 Use the prepositions from Exercise 3 to complete the text.

When you can't recycle all the waste which comes ¹_____ a big city, it's often taken away and burned ²_____ another place, usually the countryside. This creates a lot of dangerous smoke and pollution in the air. But the Amager Bakke power station in Copenhagen, Denmark does things a little differently. Three hundred lorries full of the city's waste arrive ³_____ its very modern building every day. This waste is burned, but here they immediately turn the heat ⁴_____ energy for local homes. But the power station is probably more famous for the outdoor skiing centre that was added ⁵_____ the roof. Some local people like it because they can go up ⁶_____ the top of the building after work and ski for an hour ⁷_____ dinner. It has been open for ⁸_____ three years now. It's not popular with everyone, but it's certainly original.

Grammar 2 articles

1 For each rule, write 'I' if you need an indefinite article, 'D' for a definite article and 'N' if there is no article used.

1 When we talk about something or someone we have mentioned before _____

2 When we say which thing or things we mean _____

3 When we talk about people or things in a general way _____

4 When we talk about someone or something for the first time _____

5 When we use proper names _____

6 When we talk about instruments _____

7 When the other person already knows what we are talking about _____

8 When we talk about someone's job _____

9 When we talk about the names of rivers, deserts and mountain ranges _____

10 When we talk about something that is unique _____

2 Now match the rules (1–10) in Exercise 1 with these examples.

a Then the woman walked up to us and started talking. _____

b I'm going climbing in the Andes this summer. _____

c Oranges are my favourite fruit. _____

d Did you enjoy the book? _____

e There was a young woman opposite me. _____

f My brother can play the piano. _____

g The films I like the most are her early ones. _____

h I'd like to go and see the midnight sun one day. _____

i Jenny's a teacher. _____ and _____

3 Choose the correct option to complete the sentences.

1 I have *a* / - breakfast at 7 a.m.

2 Do you know *a* / *the* time?

3 She's *a* / *the* nurse at our local hospital.

4 I have *a* / - problem I wanted to discuss with you.

5 We don't use *the* / - books or *the* / - photocopies in our class – just *a* / - materials from *the* / - internet.

6 Can I ask you *a* / *the* favour?

7 I'd love to visit *the* / - Angel Falls.

8 Fish in *the* / - Pacific are dying because of all *the* / - plastic bags in *the* / - sea.

4 Correct the mistakes with the articles where necessary. Two sentences are correct.

1 We cycled through valley before lunch.
_____

2 I'd like to go to the Moon one day.
_____

3 My brother is doctor.
_____

4 The rivers around here are so dirty.
_____

5 She plays a guitar in a band.
_____

6 That's a new head teacher at my school.
_____

5 Complete the text with *a*, *an*, *the* or –.

It's easy to set up ¹_____ local group to do something about ²_____ climate change and ³_____ environment. First you need to identify ⁴_____ exact problem you are worried about. Is it all ⁵_____ rubbish you find in ⁶_____ sea or ⁷_____ plastic that is used in ⁸_____ shops? You then need to let people know about ⁹_____ group. You could send ¹⁰_____ emails, but these days ¹¹_____ social media is better. Finally, you need to set up ¹²_____ meeting to discuss your group's name and what you want to achieve.

▶ **Grammar reference 3.3, p164 in Student's Book**

Writing
including useful expressions; planning your work; writing an email

Learning REMINDER

Including useful expressions

- Remember that common useful expressions can make an informal letter or email sound more natural.
- Start a letter or email with friendly questions and greetings, e.g. *Hi! How are you?*
- End a letter or email with friendly expressions, e.g. *Bye for now! Speak to you later.*
- Use other expressions in informal letters and emails, e.g. *Thanks for your message, I was sorry to hear about your friend, I've got some great news!*

1 Which expressions are used at the start (S) of an email and which are used at the end (E)?

1 Bye! _____
2 Bye for now _____
3 Hello _____
4 How are things? _____
5 How are you? _____
6 Keep in touch _____
7 See you soon _____
8 Write soon! _____
9 Take care. _____
10 Good to hear from you. _____

2 Read the writing task. Are the statements below true (T) or false (F)?

You have received an email from a friend. She mentions a local group that is trying to do something positive about climate change. Your friend has asked you about similar action groups in your own area.

You should

a describe a group and say what they have done in your area

b give your opinion of the group

Now write an email to reply to your friend.

1 You have to write a letter. _____
2 Your friend would like some information. _____
3 The text will be about your school. _____
4 The email will be informal. _____
5 You should say what you think about something. _____

3 Look at Jack's answer to the task in Exercise 2. Then complete his notes below.

Hi Beth

How are things? It sounds like the action group you set up is doing some really important things. Yes, we have several local groups, but the one I like best is Earth Youth Environmental Society or E.Y.E.S.

E.Y.E.S has been organising a lot of activities and projects in my area. They have also been presenting solar power projects to schools and a few have started using solar power because of them. They also organise a beach clean on the last Sunday of every month. I joined in last weekend and it was good fun.

I think it's a really cool group for young people and they're doing a lot to prevent climate change and damage to the environment.

Write again soon

Jack

> **Notes:**
>
> **Paragraph 1:** *Greeting; Tell Beth about E.Y.E.S*
>
> **Paragraph 2:** *Talk about their activities:*
> - *presenting solar power projects to schools*
> - 1 _____
>
> **Paragraph 3:** *Opinion of them:*
> - 2 _____ *and doing a lot for environment*

4 Read the Exam Reminder and complete the Exam Task. Don't forget to use the Useful Language on page 39 of your Student's Book.

Exam REMINDER

Planning your work

- Remember to plan what you are going to write.
- Read the task and underline all the key points.
- Decide how many paragraphs you need and what you want to include in each.
- Check your writing. Have you included everything? Is the order logical?

Exam TASK

Write an email (100-130 words) to a friend who has asked you to explain what your local youth group is doing to reduce waste and pollution in your area

You should mention:

- any activities that you have taken part in.
- things that you could do with your group.

Reading
understanding new words; matching sentences to gaps

1 Read the Exam Reminder. What do you need to do when you find a word you don't know?

_____

2 Read and complete the Exam Task.

Exam TASK

Matching sentences to gaps

Five sentences have been removed from the text below. For each question, choose the correct answer A–H. There are three extra sentences which you do not need to use.

A Small items like these can be difficult to find and Swenkas spend days shopping around for them.

B This is a lot of money for someone who's earning $300 or $400 a month in a factory.

C The high cost of the clothes is the reason why many people decide not to become Swenkas.

D There are important differences between the two though.

E People needed something to help them forget about these problems.

F They also travel to other areas of the country to take part in these fashion shows.

G When the show has finished, the audience votes on the best look and the winner is chosen.

H Unfortunately, there are now fewer Swenkas in Johannesburg than there used to be in the past.

Looking good
in South Africa

1 A lot of young men and women moved from the countryside to Johannesburg in the 1950s searching for a better life. However, many of them found themselves in jobs with low pay and difficult working conditions. Outside of work, these young people looked for a way to express their sense of pride and self-respect. **(1)** _____ For some, the solution was to become Swenkas. This describes a group of people who share looking confident and stylish as a hobby. Although they may not have much money they always want to look really smart and elegant. They're happy when other people look at and admire their clothes, just like the sapeurs in Kinshasa. **(2)** _____

10 For example, Swenkas are a smaller group with their own particular culture. They also have their own special look. They don't wear bright colours but prefer expensive suits, which often have the name of a famous designer on the label. There is a lot of attention to small details too, so old-fashioned hats, colourful glasses, leather shoes, gloves and big metal watches are all popular. An original handkerchief that sits in a pocket and goes well with an expensive silk tie is also essential for some. **(3)** _____ They also need to try all these things on before they finally decide on the right one to buy.

An important moment in the week is the Saturday evening fashion show, which is free to the public but not the Swenkas, who pay to enter. This money becomes the
20 winner's prize money. The aim of every well-dressed competitor is to be smarter and more fashionable than the others. Sometimes the clothes that they're wearing can cost more than $1,000. **(4)** _____ During the contest, they walk around, dance and show their new clothes. **(5)** _____ The following week, the competition takes place again with every Swenka hoping to win the prize.

Vocabulary 1 clothes and materials

1 **Choose the correct options to complete the sentences.**

1 I love your blue silk *glasses / tie*.
2 I never wear a *coat / watch* in winter here because it's warm all year.
3 I need to wear a pair of *glasses / gloves* to read.
4 I'll get a *handkerchief / button* for you. You've got a really bad cold!
5 My hands are freezing and I've left my *earrings / gloves* at home.
6 Are you sure the ticket isn't in your *pocket / tie*?
7 I need to get a new *ring / watch*. This one has stopped working.
8 I love that *bracelet / pocket*. It goes really well with your new earrings.
9 I never wear *earrings / a scarf* to work because they don't let us wear any jewellery.
10 A: I can't find my new *ring / watch*. B: Look, it's on your finger!
11 Oh no! I've lost a *ring / button* on my new jacket.
12 It's so cold. I need to get a *scarf / bracelet* to keep my neck warm.

2 **Complete the sentences with these words.**

antique	casual	fashionable	loose
old-fashioned	original	smart	tight

1 She wears formal clothes to work, but in her free-time she's very _____ — just jeans and a T-shirt.
2 This shirt is too _____ . I prefer them tighter than this.
3 You look very _____ today! Are you going to an important meeting?
4 I've never seen anything like the design on your T-shirt. It's really _____ .
5 Look at those shoes. They're so _____ . Nobody wears them anymore!
6 You're always so _____ . You're always wearing the latest styles.
7 My aunt gave me a(n) _____ ring. It's more than 100 years old.
8 These jeans are too _____ . Have you got a bigger size?

3 **Choose the correct option (a, b or c) to complete the sentences.**

1 Most shoes are made of _____ .
   a glass   b metal   c leather
2 Please clean the _____ in the windows.
   a silk   b glass   c cotton
3 People often wear _____ clothes during warm weather.
   a cotton   b metal   c plastic
4 This _____ comes from sheep in Argentina.
   a silk   b cotton   c wool
5 Knives and forks are usually made of _____ .
   a glass   b metal   c leather
6 The Swenkas like wearing expensive _____ ties.
   a silk   b leather   c wool

Grammar 1 relative clauses

1 **Underline the relative clauses in these sentences. Are they defining (D) or non-defining (N)?**

1 Jamie, who is a colleague of mine, has invited me to his party. _____

2 The new clothes shop, which is just out of town, sells all those expensive brands. _____

3 The people who live in that house are very friendly. _____

4 We use this software, which you can download for free, to write all our documents. _____

5 The restaurants that sell local food are quite popular around here. _____

6 Dino's snack bar, where we used to go at lunchtime, has just closed down. _____

2 **Choose the correct option to complete the sentences.**

1 My cousin, *who / which* lives by the sea, swims every day.

2 Do you have a dress *which / who* I can borrow for the party?

3 I think that's the boy *who / whose* parents we met on holiday.

4 Can you remember *where / which* we saw the black leather jacket?

5 Summer is the time *which / when* I travel most.

6 I'm looking for a place *where / that* sells cheap clothes.

3 **Complete the sentences with *who, which* or *whose*.**

1 Do you know _____ trainers these are?

2 Sonia, _____ only moved to this area a few years ago, is my best friend at school.

3 Have you seen the gloves _____ I was wearing earlier?

4 This new scarf, _____ my sister bought for me as a present, looks really smart.

5 That's the student _____ mum also works at the school.

6 We need a person _____ speaks really good French.

7 He bought a silk tie _____ cost $800.

8 I met the man _____ designed the watch.

Listening listening for similar words; multiple choice with six conversations

1 **Read the Exam Reminder. What words do you need to think about when you look at the questions and answer options?**

_____

2 **4.1 ▶ Listen and complete the Exam Task.**

Exam TASK

Multiple choice with six conversations

For each question, choose the correct answer, A, B or C.

1 You will hear Samir talking with a friend about a problem he had at school. How does he feel about it now?
   A angry
   B confused
   C miserable

2 You will hear two friends talking about buying things online. What does the boy never buy on the internet these days?
   A T-shirts
   B shoes
   C sports clothes

3 You will hear a woman telling a friend about an item she bought. Why did she take it back to the shop?
   A It was too loose.
   B It was too tight.
   C There was something wrong with it.

4 You will hear two friends talking about a new shop in town. What does the girl think about it?
   A She likes the fashionable clothes it sells.
   B The clothes it sells are too casual.
   C She doesn't like the clothes it sells.

5 You will hear a boy and a girl talking about a present to buy for their mum. What do they finally decide to buy?
   A a scarf
   B a coat
   C earrings

6 You will hear two friends talking about a book. What do they agree about?
   A It's boring.
   B It's too long.
   C There are too many difficult words.

▶ Grammar reference 4.1, p165 in Student's Book

Vocabulary 2 shopping; phrasal verbs (1)

1 Choose the correct option to complete the sentences.

1 Oh no, I haven't got enough *cash / receipt* to pay for my train ticket. Can you lend me some until we get home?

2 I think you should buy that coat. At that price, it's a *label / bargain*.

3 The assistant was quite rude to the *label / customer*.

4 If you're not sure how to wash it, just have a look at the *receipt / label*.

5 I need to take this shirt back to the shop and change it, but I can't find the *label / receipt*.

6 We've just booked a holiday and paid for it on our *label / credit card*.

2 Complete the text with these words.

bargain	cash	credit card	customer
label	receipt		

I'm probably not an easy ¹_____ because I'm always looking for the best possible price. I know that everybody likes to find a ²_____ , but for me it's the most important thing. I never look at the ³_____ to check what the material is or where it's made.

When I've finally decided what to buy, I always pay with ⁴_____ because I haven't got a ⁵_____ . But when I get home, I sometimes decide I don't like the T-shirt or jeans I've just bought. That's why I always keep the ⁶_____ because I'll need it to take the item back to the shop.

3 Look at the definitions on the right and complete the verbs (1–8) with the correct preposition.

1 shop _____   look for clothes in different places

2 find _____   discover something

3 pick _____   take something in your hands

4 look _____   check something with your eyes

5 wear _____   damage something by using it a lot

6 pay _____   give money for something

7 go _____   look good with other clothes

8 try _____   see if clothes look good on you

4 Use the correct form of the verbs in Exercise 3 to complete the text.

I hardly ever buy something in the first shop I go in. I like to ¹_____ for a few hours until I see something I really like. I also like to ²_____ what's on offer in different shops. I often go to the shopping centre with my friends. We always touch and ³_____ the clothes because we want to feel the quality of the material. I don't want to buy something that is going to ⁴_____ within a few weeks. I also ⁵_____ the label to check the material and see where it's made. I enjoy ⁶_____ the clothes to see if they fit and look good, but it takes me a long time to decide if I like them. I also think about the clothes I've got at home and make sure I've got something that will ⁷_____ the new clothes. When I'm happy with my choice, I go and ⁸_____ my items. I always keep the receipt because sometimes I change my mind and I want to take the clothes back to the shop.

Grammar 2 clauses with time expressions; understanding the whole meaning; open cloze

1 Choose the correct option to complete the sentences.

1 I'll call you *until / as soon as* we get there.

2 Make sure you've got everything ready *before / when* you go.

3 We won't be sure *until / as soon as* we get the email.

4 I'll tell Mark *when / until* I see him later.

5 We need to pay *until / the moment* we book the tickets.

6 I can't use the car *until / as soon as* Dad has brought it back from the garage.

7 *When / Until* you've finished, give me a call.

8 Call me *the moment / until* you've got your results.

2 Tick (✔) the sentences where both tenses are possible.

1 You can only go out when you *finish / have finished* all your homework. ☐

2 They normally call us the moment *they arrive / they've arrived.* ☐

3 I'll make you some sandwiches before you *leave / have left.* ☐

4 You need to get to the shopping centre as soon as the sales *begin / have begun.* ☐

5 Come and say goodbye before you *go / have gone.* ☐

6 As soon as they *contact / have contacted* me I'll send you a text. ☐

3 Now choose the correct option in the sentences you didn't tick in Exercise 2.

4 Choose the correct option to complete the sentences.

1 She'll only visit us when she *finishes / has finished* painting the house.

2 I'll call you when *I'm / I'll be* ready.

3 I *take / 'll take* you to your hotel after you've arrived at the airport.

4 They'll send us a copy of the file as soon as they *'ll download / 've downloaded* it.

5 Remember to sign the form before you *leave / have left.*

6 I'll only come out when I *do / 've done* all my homework.

7 We'll go to Sydney before *we visit / we've visited* Don in Cairns.

8 As soon as we hear anything, we *will let / have let* you know.

5 Read the Exam Reminder. Then read and complete the Exam Task.

Exam TASK

Open cloze
Write **one** word for each gap.

Party clothes!

It's our end-of-year party at the weekend. As soon ¹_____ I received the invitation I thought about what to wear. I've got a really nice jacket, but it doesn't go ²_____ the trousers I want to wear. I went to my favourite shopping centre and decided to stay there ³_____ I found a pair of trousers I really liked. I tried ⁴_____ at least ten pairs, but they were all ⁵_____ tight for me. It was nearly 7 p.m. and a few minutes ⁶_____ the shop closed, I finally found a pair ⁷_____ looked really good on me.

▶ Grammar reference 4.2, p165 in Student's Book

Writing
organising a story; thinking of ideas; writing a story

1 Match the first parts of the sentences 1–3 to the second parts a–c.

1 The beginning of a story ☐
2 The middle of a story ☐
3 The end of a story ☐

a explains the action in the story.
b introduces and describes the time, the place and the people in a story.
c describes the action in the story.

2 Read the writing task and then decide if the statements below are true (T) or false (F).

Your English teacher has asked you to write a story. Your story must begin with this sentence.

Alice couldn't find the bag with all her new clothes.

1 You need to write a story. _____
2 You can begin your story any way you like. _____
3 The story will be about someone who gets lost.
_____

3 Read the Exam Reminder. Then read the example story and answer the questions.

Exam REMINDER

Thinking of ideas
- Make a plan for your story before you begin writing.
- Think about the people in it and where your story takes place.
- Write down some adjectives you can use to describe the people and place(s).
- Make sure that your story has three parts: a beginning, a middle and an end.

Alice couldn't find the bag with all her new clothes. She was sure she'd put it right next to her chair when she sat down. She'd bought herself some new clothes and also a nice pair of gloves and a silk scarf for her mum's birthday before stopping to have a drink. Suddenly, Alice looked at the table next to hers. 'That's odd', she thought. 'Why's my bag over there?' Nobody was sitting at the other table. She got up and looked inside the bag but only saw a boy's T-shirt. She decided to go home. She was unhappy because she'd spent all her pocket money on her mum's presents and someone had taken them. Just as she was leaving, a boy came towards her with a shopping bag in his hand. 'Is this yours? I just realised I took it by mistake' he said. There were her new clothes and her mum's presents in the bag. 'Oh, thank you!' said Alice. 'And that must be your bag over there.'

1 Who is the main character?
_____

2 Where is the story set?
_____

3 Are there any other characters?
_____

4 Something strange happens. What s it?
_____

5 How does the story end?
_____

4 Read and complete the Exam Task. Don't forget to use the Useful Language on page 51 of your Student's Book.

Exam TASK

Writing a story

Your English teacher has asked you to write a story. Your story must begin with this sentence. *Hannah woke up and realised something was wrong.*

Write your story in about **100 words**.

Reading identifying the main message; multiple choice with five short texts

1 Read the Exam Reminder. When can you decide that an answer option is wrong?

_____

2 Read and complete the Exam Task.

Exam REMINDER

Identifying the main message

- Remember to read the texts first and think about where you would see them and what type of text each one is.
- Then look at the answer options and underline any key words.
- Read the texts again and look for similar information to the words you underlined. If you can't find any similar information in the text, that answer won't be the right option.
- Finally, check the information for the answer options you thought were possible and choose the one which answers that question best.

Exam TASK

Multiple choice with five short texts

For each question, choose the correct answer.

1

Hi Rachel

Lovely weather here in Sardinia and I'm having a great time! My accommodation is great and really modern. The flat is about 200 m from the sea. Neighbours are a bit noisy though. One of them plays the guitar until really late.

Hope the good weather lasts, but they say there will be storms from tomorrow.

Ben

Ben isn't very happy with

A the weather.
B his flat.
C the people that live near him.

2

From: Lisa
To: Sophie

Do you want to come round tomorrow and help me choose the paint for the living room in my new flat? The painter is coming and I don't want the same boring colours I have in the other rooms!

Let me know as soon as you can.

What should Sophie do?

A get in touch with Lisa
B paint Lisa's living room
C find a painter

3

Student accommodation in city centre

Not available until September

Shared kitchen plus use of washing machine (not included in monthly rent). Duvets and sheets provided.

Students

A can move into the accommodation immediately.
B won't have a kitchen.
C pay extra to use the washing machine.

4

Hi Anahita

Thanks for waiting for the parcel to arrive. Remember your keys and please lock the door when you leave.

Dad

Why has Anahita's dad written the note?

A to remind her to take her keys
B to remind her to wait for a parcel
C to remind her that the door is locked

5

Hi Alex

Thanks for lending me your ladder the other day. I finished the job in no time at all! Let me know when I can get it back to you. Maybe one evening next week?

Liam

Liam

A didn't use the ladder in the end.
B found the ladder useful.
C wants to bring it back this evening.

Vocabulary 1 housing; household objects (1)

1 Choose the correct option to complete the sentences.

1 I live in a large *accommodation / apartment block* in the city centre.
2 My dream is to have a beautiful *cottage / flat* in the countryside.
3 I live with three *neighbours / flatmates* of the same age.
4 My cousin buys and sells *rent / property* in New Zealand.
5 I love this place, but the *property / rent* s too high, so I'll have to find somewhere cheaper.
6 I'm moving to Spain this year, but it's really hard to find cheap *accommodation / apartment block*.
7 I live in a small flat by myself, but my *neighbours / flatmates* are really noisy.
8 It's expensive to live here, so I live in a *cottage / flat* in a big apartment block.

2 Complete the text with these words.

accommodation	apartment block	cottage
flat	flatmate	property	rent

My life has completely changed in the last 18 months. I used to live with my parents in a beautiful
¹ _____ in the countryside outside Budapest. It was so peaceful. Then I found my first job in the city. ² _____ prices are very high in Budapest, so I had to move into a small one-bedroom ³ _____ . It's in a(n) ⁴ _____ in the Kispest area of the city, which is not far from where I work. The ⁵ _____ is quite high, but the company gives us some money for our ⁶ _____ and that helps a lot. But the best thing? It's great not having a ⁷ _____ . It means I can choose what I want to watch on TV!

3 Choose the correct option to complete the sentences.

1 Be careful when you go in. The *ladder / ceiling* is very low in this room.
2 Do you have a *kettle / bin* for all this rubbish?
3 I can't reach those boxes up there. Have you got a small *ladder / bucket* I can use?
4 It's hot in here. Let's go out on to the *balcony / shelf*.
5 Please put your dirty clothes in the *dishwasher / washing machine*.
6 You can heat the milk in the *fridge / microwave*.
7 Do you have a(n) *brush / iron* to clean the floor?
8 If you turn the *freezer / kettle* on, I'll make some tea.
9 Your bike is in the *garage / balcony*.
10 Make sure you put the milk back in the *oven / fridge*.

4 Choose the correct options (a–c) to complete the sentences.

1 That book is too high up. I need to use a
  a shelf. b bucket. c ladder.
2 If you want to keep the prawns fresh, you should keep them in the
  a fridge. b microwave. c washing machine.
3 I hate washing up. I really wish my flat had a
  a bucket. b dishwasher. c freezer.
4 I'd like some tea. Is there any water in the
  a iron? b kettle? c bucket?
5 Please can you put these books back on the
  a balcony. b bin. c shelf.
6 I bought a new bike, but I need to keep it in the
  a freezer. b garage. c balcony.
7 A potato takes about ten minutes to cook in a
  a fridge. b microwave. c dishwasher.
8 Before you bake a cake, you need to turn on the
  a oven. b kitchen. c iron.
9 Sal helped me do some chores yesterday, but she burned her hand on the
  a ceiling. b bucket. c iron.
10 I need to wash the floor, so please could you fill up a
  a bucket. b freezer. c bin.

Grammar 1 *will; be going to*

1 Choose the correct option to complete the sentences.

1 My sister *will / is going to* study medicine.

2 Oh no! Joe *will / is going to* fall off his bike.

3 It's been snowing all night, so we *won't / aren't going to* visit Leah this morning.

4 *I'll / I'm going to* get really angry if you don't tell me right now.

5 *Will you / Are you going to* be as quiet as possible when you come back tonight, please?

6 I expect they *won't / aren't going to* arrive on time as usual.

7 I hope we *will / are going to* see you later.

8 **A:** Oh no! We need more paper for the printer.
   B: It's OK, *I'll get / I'm going to get* some later.

9 My sister *will / is going to* be sixteen in June.

10 Can you lend me your bike? *I'll / I'm going to* bring it back tomorrow, I promise.

2 Complete the conversation with the correct form of *will* or *be going to* and the verbs in brackets.

Carla: So, when ¹ _____ (you / move) house, Juan?

Juan: Next month. The school in Buenos Aires ² _____ (call) me next week to tell me when I can start. I think it ³ _____ (be) at the beginning of September, but I'm not sure.

Carla: What ⁴ _____ (you / do) with the flat you're living in?

Juan: Well I ⁵ _____ (not / sell) it, that's for sure. I hope I ⁶ _____ (come) back to live here one day.

Carla: Are you happy that you ⁷ _____ (live) in a big city? There are so many people in Buenos Aires.

Juan: Well, yes and no. I hope everything ⁸ _____ (be) OK, but I think I ⁹ _____ (find) it difficult at the start. Anyway, I must go. The ticket office ¹⁰ _____ (close) in a couple of minutes and I need to buy my train ticket for tomorrow …

Carla: OK. I ¹¹ _____ (call) you before you leave.

Listening *identifying opinion; multiple choice with one conversation*

1 Read the Exam Reminder. Why do you need to be careful when people give their opinion?

_____

2 **5.1 ▶** **Listen and complete the Exam Task.**

Exam TASK

Multiple choice with one conversation

For each question, choose the correct answer A, B or C.

You will hear a radio interview with an architect who is talking about student accommodation.

1 Jenny believes that
   A students are too young to be interested in where they're living.
   B it's too expensive to design good quality student accommodation.
   C it's possible to design nice but cheap accommodation.

2 Jenny thinks the *Spaceboxes*
   A have nice colours and are comfortable.
   B aren't nice to look at but are practical.
   C are small for two students sharing a room.

3 The students that Jenny talked to
   A all liked their accommodation.
   B generally didn't like their accommodation.
   C had good and bad opinions about their accommodation.

4 Jenny thinks that
   A local people were right about *Spaceboxes*.
   B the *Spaceboxes* use space in a clever way.
   C there should be somewhere for students to spend time together.

5 Jenny says that the *Spaceboxes*
   A have a shower for every five students.
   B have a washing machine on every floor.
   C offer more facilities for students than typical student accommodation.

6 What does Jenny say about the cost of the *Spaceboxes*?
   A They are more expensive because they have individual bathrooms.
   B They are cheaper than similar apartments in the city thanks to efficient heating.
   C They are more expensive than normal apartments but they are much warmer.

▶ Grammar references 5.1 and 5.2, p166 in Student's Book

Vocabulary 2 household objects (2); home expressions

1 Choose the correct option to complete the sentences.

1 Let's use a thinner *pillow / duvet* because it's getting warm at night now.

2 Have you got a *duvet / cushion*? This chair isn't very comfortable.

3 They change the *sheets / cushions* every day in this hotel.

4 Is it possible to have an extra *pillow / cushion* on the bed? I normally sleep with two at home.

5 I keep all my T-shirts and socks in a *bookcase / chest of drawers* near the window.

6 Can you hang these jackets in the *chest of drawers / wardrobe*?

7 Could I have an extra *pillow / blanket*? It's starting to get cold at night.

8 You'll find the dictionary on the top shelf of the *bookcase / chest of drawers*.

2 Match the verb on the left (1–6) with a word or phrase on the right (a–f).

1	do ☐	**a**	away
2	make ☐	**b**	your room
3	tidy ☐	**c**	a break
4	have ☐	**d**	a noise
5	move ☐	**e**	a seat
6	take ☐	**f**	the housework

3 Complete the sentences with *have, do, make, move, tidy* or *take*.

1 I always _____ my bed before leaving for school.

2 My neighbours are going to _____ house in June.

3 Please _____ a seat and we'll start the meeting in a few minutes.

4 I'll just _____ a quick shower before dinner.

5 We try to _____ the whole house at least once a week.

6 When the dishwasher is broken, my parents ask me to _____ the washing up.

7 Try not to _____ a mess in your room. I've spent all morning cleaning.

8 Would you like to _____ a coffee while you're waiting?

4 Complete the text using one of the verbs in the first box and a word or phrase from the second box.

do	have	make	move	take	tidy

a break	a coffee	a lot of noise	a shower
house	my bed	the housework	up
the washing up			

My week is pretty busy. I get up at 6 o'clock every morning. I try not to ¹ _____ because everybody's still asleep and I don't want to wake anyone up. I always ² _____ before I leave because it makes my bedroom look a bit tidier.

I work all morning and only ³ _____ around 1 p.m. when I go and get a sandwich with my colleagues.

I get a bit tired around mid-afternoon, so I
⁴ _____ from the café near the office – a cappuccino usually. When I get home, I normally ⁵ _____ . I really need one after travelling home on a hot and crowded bus.

I help prepare dinner and then I ⁶ _____ because we haven't got a dishwasher. It doesn't take long to ⁷ _____ the kitchen. But I haven't got enough energy to ⁸ _____ as that takes too long. But that's not a problem at the moment because we're going to ⁹ _____ next month and there are boxes everywhere. I'll be sad to leave this area after living here for more than twenty years.

Grammar 2 future plans and events; future predictions

1 Choose the correct option to complete the sentences.

1 Hurry up! The film *starts / is going to start* at 8 p.m.

2 *We're going to decide / We're deciding* on the exact date of the holiday later in the week.

3 My lessons *finish / are going to finish* at 4 p.m., so I can meet you after that.

4 What time *does your plane leave / is your plane going to leave*?

5 Sorry I can't meet you later. *I go / I'm going* to the dentist this afternoon.

6 *We're meeting / We meet* outside the cinema at 7 p.m. if you want to come.

7 My parents *buy / are going to buy* me a new bike for my birthday.

8 Sorry I can't come out tonight. My favourite TV programme *is / is being* on at nine o'clock.

9 What time *do you go / are you going* to the party this evening?

10 One day *I'm visiting / I'm going to visit* my relatives in Canada.

2 Choose the correct option to complete the sentences.

1 Sam *might / will* be late this evening. It depends what time his meeting finishes.

2 If it's like last year, there *will be / are going to be* lots of people at the concert.

3 She *will / might* probably come and visit us this weekend.

4 They say it *will / might* snow tomorrow, but nothing is certain at the moment.

5 I'm sure you *will / are going to* get that job.

6 I hope this party *might / will* be better than the last one.

3 Complete the text with the correct future form of these verbs.

be (x2)	go	have to	meet	not/live
start	stay	study	visit	wait

My big sister [1] _____ to university for the first time tomorrow and tonight she
[2] _____ all her friends after dinner to say goodbye.

She [3] _____ in the university itself because she's renting a flat with two other friends in a nearby town.

She [4] _____ French and Italian. She found out from last year's students that the course
[5] _____ quite difficult, but she's looking forward to it. She [6] _____ read lots of books, but she loves that. Her lessons
[7] _____ on Monday and I think she
[8] _____ a little bit nervous on Sunday evening.

I [9] _____ her in her first term, but I know that other friends [10] _____ with her, too, so I expect I [11] _____ until the second term before going.

Grammar references 5.3 and 5.4, p166 in Student's Book

Writing
responding to news; using appropriate language: writing an email

1 Read the writing task and answer the questions.

You have received an email from your cousin, Laurie, who is moving to another city to start university.

Write a letter in reply to Laurie.

Hi Nathan

Congratulate her

How are you? I'm in Edinburgh! I got a place at university here and I'm really excited!

My course starts in three weeks and I'm here looking for a flat to rent. Everything is pretty expensive, so I need cheap furniture. Can you help? Have you got anything you don't need? If so, I can come and pick it up.

Say what furniture I can give her

When the flat is ready, I'd like you to come and stay. I'd love to see you and show you around.

Yes, definitely …

Let me know when you can come and I'll pick you up at the station.

Say when

Bye for now

Laurie

---

1 Where is Laurie studying? _____
2 What does she need? _____
3 What does she offer to do? _____

2 Read Nathan's reply and answer the questions.

Hi Laurie

Great news! I've heard that Edinburgh is beautiful. You're so lucky!

I've got a small chest of drawers and a microwave you can have when you find a flat.

I'd love to visit you. I've got some free time at the end of October. I can come on Friday 28th and leave on Monday 31st. Would that be OK?

See you soon

Nathan

---

1 Has Nathan responded to all of Laurie's email?
_____

2 Has Nathan replied to Laurie's questions in the same order as Laurie asked them?
_____

3 Has Nathan written in a formal or an informal style?
_____

3 Read the Exam Reminder. Why do you need to think about who you are writing to?

_____

4 Read and complete the Exam Task below. Don't forget to use the Useful Language on page 63 of your Student's Book.

Exam TASK

Writing an email

Read this email from your English-speaking friend Ekaterina and the notes you have made. Write your email to Ekaterina using all the notes.

Hi there

That sounds cool …

How are you? Guess what? I'm going to New York for two months in July. I'm going to do an English course, but I'm not sure where to stay. Should I stay with a family or in special student accommodation near the school?

Say which I think …

Yes, look at …

Do you have any guide books or information about New York? I'd like to start preparing in the next few days. It'd be really good to have a video call with you. Have you got some free time for that?

Yes, suggest time

Ekaterina

Write your answer in about **100 words**.

Reading identifying the key points; matching people to texts

1 Read the Exam Reminder. Do you need to match all of the texts to a description?

_____

A new you?

Do you want to try something different from the usual game of football or tennis? Here are eight unusual but cool sports that you might like to try.

A Bandy

1 Do you fancy playing bandy? It's a mix between ice hockey, field hockey and football. It's popular in Russia and Scandinavia. You play outdoors on ice and there are eleven players in each team. You try to hit a small round ball into a small goal with a stick. If you like football, you'll love bandy because the rules are exactly the same.

B Lacrosse

If you want to play lacrosse, you'll need a field, some special sticks with nets, gloves, a helmet and a few
10 good friends. Lacrosse is a great team sport and there are different types. In some, you can have contact with another player but, in others, only the sticks can be in contact with each other. You can play either of these indoors or outdoors depending on the weather.

C White water canoeing

This is a great sport for a person who loves to be alone with nature and is looking for some real adventure. Most people know white water rafting, but that's for groups. Here it's just you, your strength, your skill and some really fast water. You'll need a swimming
20 costume, life jacket and a really good helmet.

D Climbing

Climbing is a good way to really escape from everything … and everyone. Climbing is a special skill and if you practise on an indoor rock face you'll soon

be ready to try something more difficult. When you're up by yourself at 3,000 m with blue skies all around it's the best feeling in the world!

E Sepak Takraw

There's a big net and two teams, one on each side. If you've played volleyball, this might sound familiar. Well, in this sport you don't score points with your
30 hands and arms but just your feet, so you need good football skills. There are five players on each side and it's the perfect winter sport for anyone who likes doing indoor activities and meeting new people.

F Cross-training

Want to try a bit of everything? Cross-training is perfect for anybody who gets bored just doing one sport all the time. In cross-training you can choose a fitness programme that's perfect for you. For example, do fifteen minutes on the track then a fast bike ride. The important thing is that you do lots of different
40 activities in a thirty-minute or one-hour workout.

G Walking basketball

If the gym isn't for you or you can't run fast, try walking basketball. You just walk with the ball and pass it to someone in the team or try to score a basket in the usual way. It's great for older people who want to keep active and meet others.

H Tai Chi

This is a bit like karate, but it teaches you how to defend yourself rather than attack. It's good for people who have a lot of stress in their lives as our instructors will show you how to really relax. We meet in the gym
50 on Saturdays and Sundays and you'll have the chance to practise with a small group of friendly people.

Vocabulary 1

2 Read and complete the Exam Task.

Exam TASK

Matching people to texts

These people all want to try a new sport. Read the descriptions of eight sports. Decide which sport / activity would be the most suitable for the people below.

1  Maggie is 50 and has always loved athletics, but she recently injured her knee, so needs a new activity where she doesn't have to run too much. She would also like to make some new friends. _____

2  Lori is 17 and a very active person. She already does a number of water sports like water-skiing and paddleboarding and is an excellent swimmer. She has a real sense of adventure and loves exciting sports activities. _____

3  Matt is 20. He lives in the mountains and does a lot of ice-skating competitions in the winter. As he spends a lot of time indoors training by himself for these, he would like to do an open-air team activity. _____

4  Philippe is 25 and loves to go to the mountains at the weekend. He likes walking there, but generally prefers adventure sports. His job is stressful and he also wants something to do by himself after work. _____

5  Suela is 35 and loves team sports. She used to play women's football. She stopped because she didn't like training in the cold in winter. She wants to keep a good level of fitness and to make some new friends if possible. _____

1 Choose the correct option to complete the sentences.

1 I love to *go / do* swimming early in the morning.
2 Shall we *do / play* tennis in the afternoon?
3 My sister *does / goes* athletics every weekend.
4 My friend and I *go / do* running every evening.
5 I *play / do* judo with a teacher every week.
6 I never learned to *play / do* basketball at school.
7 My parents *do / go* yoga most evenings.

2 Read the Exam Reminder. What do you need to do with the options?

Exam REMINDER

Finding the wrong options

- Get a general idea of the meaning by quickly reading the text.
- Read it again and stop at each gap. Look at the four options. Try to find words that clearly don't go in the gap and cross them out.
- When you've finished, go back and check all your answers one final time.

3 Read and complete the Exam Task.

Exam TASK

Multiple-choice cloze

For each question, choose the correct answer A, B, C or D.

Did you know that when people began playing football there were several hundred ¹ _____ on each side and no ² _____ in which to score? There were just lots of jackets that people put on the ground!

Nearly all sports started out in the streets because there were no ³ _____ places to play sports.

When people first played tennis in 1526 CE they used to throw the ball and not use a ⁴ _____ like now. And in the early Olympics, ⁵ _____ didn't run on expensive ⁶ _____ like they do today. They just ran across ordinary ground.

1 A riders   B players   C matches   D goals
2 A courts   B tracks   C goal posts   D baskets
3 A inside   B interior   C internal   D indoor
4 A racket   B bat   C stick   D goal
5 A players   B riders   C athletes   D individual
6 A courts   B tracks   C pitches   D games

Grammar 1 zero and first conditional; *unless*

1 Choose the correct option to complete the sentences.

1 If you *train / will train* hard, you might win the competition.
2 If the court *is / will be* wet, we'll play tennis indoors.
3 I *call / 'll call* you if I decide to go swimming.
4 If you *are / will be* late, we might miss the train.
5 If you leave for the stadium now, there *might not / isn't* be too much traffic.
6 If I have time, I *go / 'll go* to the gym later.
7 I *leave / 'll leave* as soon as Deepak arrives.
8 When I eat ice cream, I *will get / get* a headache.

2 Complete the sentences with the correct form of the verb in brackets.

1 If you _____ (train) really hard, you _____ (run) faster than Eddie.
2 If the ball _____ (bounce) twice in tennis, you _____ (lose) the point.
3 We might have to play indoors if the weather _____ (not / get) better.
4 When we _____ (score) a goal, we always _____ (celebrate).
5 If it _____ (not / rain) later, I _____ (go) running.
6 If you _____ (break) this racket, I _____ (not / buy) you another one!
7 You _____ (feel) better if you _____ (not eat) junk food.
8 You _____ (damage) your racket if you _____ (hold) it like that.

3 Read the pairs of sentences. Do they mean the same (S) or something different (D)?

1 a You can't come in unless you pay €5.
  b You can come in if you pay €5. _____
2 a We'll go home unless it stops raining soon.
  b If it stops raining soon, we'll go home. _____
3 a Unless I find a comfortable pair of shoes, I won't go running.
  b I'll go running if I find a comfortable pair of shoes. _____

Listening checking spelling; gap fill

1 Read the Exam Reminder. What kind of words does the speaker usually spell?

_____

2 6.1 ▶ Listen and complete the Exam Task.

Exam TASK

Gap fill

You will listen to information about a race in Patagonia. Listen and write the correct information for each question. You need to write a short answer (one, two or three words), a date, a number or a time.

Patagonian Expedition Race	
Race created by Stjepan	1 _____ .
First race in February	2 _____ .
Teams come from	3 _____ .
Race goes through	4 _____ forest.
Shortest race:	5 _____ kilometres in 2004.
Longest race:	1,112 kilometres in 2007.
Goals of race:	• organise exciting competition
	• 6 _____ in the area

↻ Grammar references 6.1 and 6.2, p166–167 in Student's Book

Vocabulary 2 sports clothes; verb + noun collocations; word building

1 **Complete the sentences with these words.**

| gloves | helmet | ice skates |
| swimming costume | tracksuit | trainers |

1 If you have a good quality _____ , you can use it to train in the pool for a few years.

2 Footballers normally wear a _____ when they're warming up before a game.

3 People who go cycling and skiing need to wear a _____ to protect their head if they fall.

4 If you go to the gym, you can't wear your regular outdoor shoes. You have to wear a clean pair of _____ .

5 There's a frozen river in the city centre in winter, so we often take our _____ and enjoy ourselves for a few hours.

6 If you go jogging early in the morning in winter, remember to take some _____ in case your hands get cold.

2 **Complete the sentences with the correct form of these expressions.**

do a workout	enter a competition	hit a ball
join a club	practise a skill	ride a horse
sail a boat	score a goal	

1 I've just _____ where a friend of mine is already a member.

2 It took me a long time to learn to _____ because I was afraid of falling off.

3 We _____ in the last minute and won the match.

4 If you want to _____ in the sea, you need to do a course and get a licence.

5 My ice-skating teacher always makes me _____ that I will need in the next competition.

6 When you play cricket and baseball, you have to _____ as far as possible and then run.

7 This evening I'm going to _____ that I found online. If you want to join me, bring your tracksuit and trainers.

8 After six months of practising table tennis at home I finally decided to _____ in May.

3 **Complete the blog with these words.**

competitively	competitors	dangerous
fit	fitness	gloves	professional
strength	strengthen	tracksuit	trainers

Interested in starting running? Want to become a better athlete? Here are my top tips for new runners.

Tip 1 For any athlete, a good level of 1 _____ is essential. If you want to run a 10 km race but have never run before it'll take you at least six months before you can do that 2 _____ . You'll need to increase the 3 _____ of the muscles in your legs over many months. It's important to 4 _____ the muscles in your back too.

Tip 2 Have the right equipment. A comfortable 5 _____ is great, especially in winter, but you definitely shouldn't use the 6 _____ you wear to school every day. You need proper running shoes ... and they're expensive! A pair of 7 _____ is also really useful to stop your hands from freezing in winter!

Tip 3 It's 8 _____ to start running without warming up. Look at the 9 _____ before any big race. They all do some gentle warm-up exercises before they start.

Follow these basic tips and you'll soon start to feel really 10 _____ and be able to run just like a 11 _____ .

Grammar 2 second conditional

1 Choose the correct option to complete the sentences.

1 If I *were / would be* you, I'd join a local diving club.
2 If I *know / knew* the answer to your question, I'd tell you.
3 If the weather *is / was* better, we could go out.
4 I'm sure the teacher would help you with that exercise if you *ask / asked* her.
5 If you *study / studied* a bit harder, you could do better in tests.
6 If you *get / got* up a bit earlier, you wouldn't be late for school all the time.

2 Complete the sentences with the correct form of these verbs.

buy	do	have	not be able
not help	wear		

1 I _____ a new tracksuit if I were you. That one's getting really old.
2 If he _____ more time, my brother would join a swimming club.
3 If there wasn't such a good sports centre, I _____ to play so regularly.
4 If they _____ a proper workout every morning, they'd get really fit.
5 If you _____ gloves when you ran, your hands wouldn't get so cold.
6 If you said that to them, it _____ the situation at all.

3 Rewrite the sentences using the second conditional.

1 I don't like swimming, so I don't go to the pool very often.

_____

2 My sister doesn't train hard, so she doesn't get into the school team.

_____

3 The rider is not very good, so his horse won't win the race.

_____

4 My brother doesn't study, so he doesn't get good results.

_____

5 We don't concentrate during matches, so we don't score many points.

_____

6 We don't do any workouts, so we're not fit.

_____

4 Complete the conversation with the correct form of the verbs in brackets.

Emilio: Hi Rosa, it looks like you've enjoyed your run. Are you training for something?

Rosa: Hi Emilio. Yes, I've got a competition soon. If I ¹ _____ (have) a bit more time, I could prepare for it properly. I haven't got a coach at the moment and that's a problem too.

Emilio: If I ² _____ (be) you, I'd try to find one. If you ³ _____ (find) someone to train with, it'd be much easier for you.

Rosa: I know, but I'm afraid that a coach ⁴ _____ (not / be) pleased if I didn't spend every evening on the track. You know I've got lots of school work to do as well.

Emilio: That's true. ⁵ _____ (you / prefer) it if we did some running together?

Rosa: Of course, I'd love it if you ⁶ _____ (can) find the time. Thanks, Emilio.

Grammar reference 6.3, p167 in Student's Book

Writing giving reasons and examples; organising your essay; writing an opinion essay

1 Look at the following task and then read the example essay. How many main points does the writer use to support the opinion they give at the beginning?

_____

> Do you think sport is important for people of all ages, not just the young? Explain why / why not.

I believe that sport is important for people of all ages, not just young people. First, sport keeps people active and this is more important for older people who have greater health problems. Moreover, if they don't do any sport, they might just sit and watch TV all day.

In my opinion, sport also helps people use their brains. One example of this is tennis. You have to make quick decisions and think carefully where to hit the ball.

In addition, sport is a social activity. Many elderly people say they are lonely. When you join a team, you can make friends. Furthermore, you can eat and chat together after a game.

To sum up, sport is good for everybody, but particularly for older people. In my view, we should encourage people of all ages to play sport.

2 Read the essay again. Tick (✓) the things that the writer mentions in the essay.

1 sport is quite a lonely activity _____
2 sport is good for your health _____
3 sport is not just physical but mental activity _____
4 you can meet new people by doing sport _____
5 sport is good for everybody _____
6 sport centres should be free for elderly people _____
7 sport is a social activity _____

3 Now find and underline expressions in the essay that …

1 give the writer's opinion
2 give an example to support an opinion
3 add another point
4 conclude the writer's opinion

4 Read the Exam Reminder and complete the sentence.

In an opinion essay, you should include at least _____ reasons to support your opinion.

5 Read and complete the Exam Task. Don't forget to use the Useful Language on page 75 of your Student's Book.

Exam TASK

'There should be at least two or three lessons on sport and physical education every week in school'.

- Write an essay on whether you agree or disagree with the statement above.
- Give examples to support your opinion.

Write your essay in about **100 words**.

Reading understanding attitudes and opinions; multiple choice with one text

1 Read the Exam Reminder. What words may help you understand the writer's opinion?

In search of real eco-tourism

1 **M**ore and more people know about eco-tourism thanks to traditional and social media. A lot of companies now say they offer sustainable tourism, but how do people know if they are really buying a true eco-friendly holiday?

So, what can people do to check? First of all, they should be careful when researching their trip online. The main travel booking sites now have 'green' travel options while well-known search engines
10 have flight searches that show you how to offset the environmental cost of your flight. But can you really trust them? Companies pay money to be among the first results of these searches and will put words like 'green' and 'eco-friendly' on their sites just to get more clicks and, as a result, more business.

The answer could be to use travel sites which really are eco-friendly. For example, sites like these give most of the money they receive from advertising to tree-planting projects around the world. There are
20 now four million new trees thanks to this. These sites check hotels and campsites to compare their facilities and to find the most environmentally friendly options for you. They don't include places with a poor carbon footprint and will look only for holidays that really protect the environment. Some will also give money to environmental groups every time you make a booking. You can even choose who gets the money, which is great.

Other sites do even more and only work with hotels
30 that try to balance out their negative effects on the environment and work to reduce their CO_2. Some of these companies invest part of the money they make in environmental projects in countries around the world. They also give travellers the chance to give their hotel accommodation a score depending on how 'green' they think it really is.

Flying is of course one of the worst things for the environment and you'll never completely offset the carbon it produces. But at the same time, you
40 want to see the world and also to save money when you fly, don't you? The only way to try to fly sustainably is to use special sites that really look for the greenest, quickest and cheapest flights available. For example, visitors can find the airline that takes the most direct route to their destination and uses the most energy-efficient planes. But you have to be honest with yourself. Unless the technology completely changes, perhaps the only real way to fly sustainably is not to fly at all.

2 Read and complete the Exam Task.

Exam TASK

Multiple choice with one text

For each question, choose the correct answer
A, B, C or D.

1 The writer believes that
 A there is growing interest in eco-tourism.
 B the quality of eco-tourism is getting better.
 C people know what kind of holiday they are getting with eco-tourism.
 D all holiday companies are becoming more environmentally friendly.
2 In the writer's opinion,
 A the main travel sites help people make the right choices.
 B it's better to pay to get the best information about eco-friendly holidays.
 C the information on main travel sites may not be reliable.
 D people need to compare the results of two or three of the main travel sites before choosing.
3 Eco-friendly search engines
 A have no advertising.
 B make no money from their sites.
 C decide which charities to give money to when you book.
 D only offer certain types of holidays to users.
4 The article says that some sites
 A try to reduce a hotel's carbon footprint.
 B help people in other parts of the world.
 C give their hotels a score on how environmentally friendly they are.
 D only offer holidays in poor countries.
5 The writer thinks
 A travellers can offset their CO_2 on flights if they look carefully at different options.
 B people are not worried about cost if they think their flight is environmentally friendly.
 C it's possible to choose an airline that is better for the environment than others.
 D people should save money by not travelling by air.
6 What would be a good ending for this article?
 A In the end, travelling is always bad for the environment because of the CO_2 it produces. It may be better to stay at home if you can.
 B So choose carefully when you are trying to find an eco-friendly travel option. You may end up doing more damage to the environment than you imagine.
 C In the end, travellers can help the environment by paying extra for the holidays they choose.
 D The main search engines are therefore the first place you should look for eco-friendly holiday and flight options.

Vocabulary 1 travel

1 Choose the correct option to complete the sentences.

1 I don't think they use the same *visa / currency* as we do, so pay for it with your credit card instead.
2 You will need to show your passport when we get to our final *fare / destination*.
3 I don't think I've got enough money for the train *fare / reservation* home.
4 Don't take too much *baggage / currency* with you. Just one small suitcase is enough.
5 We couldn't eat there because we didn't have a *visa / reservation* and the restaurant was full.
6 You'll need a *visa / reservation* in your passport if you want to visit that country.
7 They normally stop all the cars and passengers at the *border / journey*.
8 It's a long *journey / reservation*, but you'll be happy when you finally get there.

2 Complete the sentences with the circled words from Exercise 1.

1 I can't remember if you need a _____ to eat in that restaurant. I'll call just in case.
2 If you have a tourist _____ n your passport, they will let you stay for one month.
3 I never take much _____ when I travel abroad – just a small backpack.
4 If you travel after ten in the morning, the train _____ is much cheaper.
5 There is a lot of traffic at the _____ between Italy and Croatia.
6 The _____ was quick and easy as there were so few cars on the road.
7 When I go to another country, I normally take my credit card and a small amount of local _____ .
8 If the ticket office is closed, you can pay at your _____ .

3 Choose the correct option to complete the sentences.

1 When I got to the gate at the airport, I couldn't find my *boarding pass / check out*.
2 There are no trains from the airport. You'll have to take the *customs / coach*.
3 I asked for a *double room / reception*, but they only had singles left.
4 We took the wrong road at the big *traffic jam / roundabout*.
5 I bought these headphones at the *duty-free / check out* shop at the airport.
6 There was a big *traffic jam / roundabout* just before the airport and we missed our flight

Grammar 1 question tags; subject and object questions

1 Choose the correct option to complete the sentences.

1 You don't really want to do that, *do / don't* you?
2 You'll write to me sometimes, *don't / won't* you?
3 The food's bad here, *isn't / wasn't* it?
4 You wanted this map, *won't / didn't* you?
5 We've sent you photos of the party, *didn't / haven't* we?
6 This is a really nice beach, *isn't / doesn't* it?

2 Complete the sentences with the correct question tag.

1 That wasn't a good idea, _____ ?
2 Your brother didn't pass his exam, _____ ?
3 We couldn't cancel the flight, _____ ?
4 They aren't going to finish on time, _____ ?
5 You're in your final year of school, _____ ?
6 We saw a really good film last night, _____ ?

3 Read the sentences and the questions. Are they subject (S) or object (O) questions?

1 Lia paid for the train fare.
   Who paid for the train fare? _____
2 The students did a project on eco-tourism.
   What did the students do? _____
3 Mandy told us about the visa.
   Who told you about the visa? _____
4 It wasn't me.
   Who booked a single instead of a double room?
   _____

4 Write the subject or object question.

1 Wilhelm has visited Spain. (subject question)
   Who _____ ?
2 He met somebody last night. (object question)
   Who _____ ?
3 My aunt is coming to stay. (subject question)
   Who _____ ?
4 She sold her smartphone to someone. (object question)
   Who _____ ?
5 Dani went to the cinema with Ava and Rico. (subject question)
   Who _____ ?

Listening matching all parts of the option; multiple choice with six conversations

1 Read the Exam Reminder. How many options do you have for each question?

_____

Exam REMINDER

Matching all parts of the option

- You will listen to six short conversations. The exam task will explain the context for each conversation. You then need to read a question and three possible answers.
- When you read the context and the questions, think about what words you will hear.
- Listen carefully to the meaning of the conversation. All parts of the answer must match.

2 **7.1 ▶** Listen and complete the Exam Task.

Exam TASK

Multiple choice with six conversations

For each question, choose the correct answer, A, B or C.

1 You will hear two friends talking about a flight. What is Kath's opinion of the flight?
   A too expensive
   B uncomfortable
   C very relaxing
2 You will hear Ellie telling a friend about her last holiday. What does she say about it?
   A It was calm and relaxing.
   B It was tiring and stressful.
   C It was too long.
3 You will hear two friends talking about a trip. Why did the police stop the man at the border?
   A He had too much local currency.
   B He'd forgotten his passport.
   C He didn't have the right visa.
4 You will hear two friends talking about a school trip. What was good about Mitch's trip?
   A the places they visited
   B the food
   C the accommodation
5 You will hear two friends talking about a recent concert. How did the girl get home?
   A by bus
   B by taxi
   C on foot
6 You will hear Eve talking to a friend about her holiday. What did she think of the campsite?
   A clean but crowded
   B uncomfortable in the evening
   C expensive and dirty

↻ Grammar references 7.1 and 7.2, p167 in Student's Book

Vocabulary 2 holiday accommodation; travel collocations; adjectives for travel

1 Match the descriptions to these names of holiday accommodation.

cabin	campsite	holiday home	hostel	hotel

1 A place to put up a tent. _____
2 A cheap place where you might stay in a room with others. _____
3 A house or villa that you live in while you're on holiday. _____
4 A general name for a place where you can sleep and often eat all your meals. _____
5 A small place to spend your holidays, often found in the country or in a campsite. _____

2 Complete the sentences with these words and a preposition.

a car	board	foot	sea	the airport
the bus stop				

1 We decided to go to the shops _____ as we both like walking.
2 The plane was quite empty. There were only around twenty people _____ .
3 It's nice to travel _____ , but the waves can make some people feel sick.
4 They met us _____ when our plane arrived.
5 Let's catch the number 32 at midday. I'll meet you _____ .
6 I don't like sitting _____ when it's really hot and you're in a traffic jam.

3 Choose the correct option to complete the sentences.

1 I really need a nice *relaxing / exciting* holiday where I just sit and do nothing all day.
2 Being in a busy airport can be quite *calm / stressful* especially when you're late for a flight.
3 Arriving in a new place is *crowded / exciting* as you don't know what to expect.
4 After two weeks of holiday I normally feel very *calm / noisy* and nothing worries me.
5 The hotel was so *crowded / comfortable*. I think I'll go back there next year.
6 The hostel was quite nice, but it was on a very *noisy / stressful* road, so I couldn't sleep at night.
7 I try not to go on holiday in August because the beaches are so *crowded / exciting*.
8 I love this place because it's so *calm / lively*. The shops and restaurants are open until late.

4 Complete the text with these words and expressions.

at the airport	at the bus stop	by air
by sea	crowded	holiday home
on board	on holiday	on time	relaxing

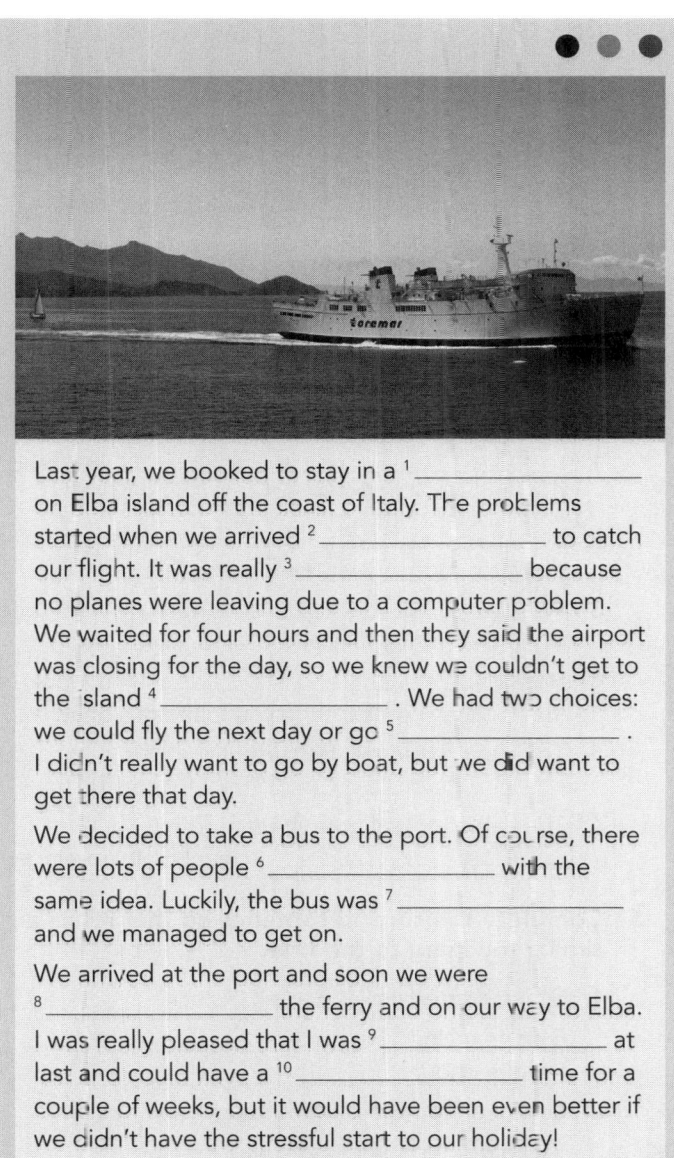

Last year, we booked to stay in a ¹_____ on Elba island off the coast of Italy. The problems started when we arrived ²_____ to catch our flight. It was really ³_____ because no planes were leaving due to a computer problem. We waited for four hours and then they said the airport was closing for the day, so we knew we couldn't get to the island ⁴_____ . We had two choices: we could fly the next day or go ⁵_____ . I didn't really want to go by boat, but we did want to get there that day.

We decided to take a bus to the port. Of course, there were lots of people ⁶_____ with the same idea. Luckily, the bus was ⁷_____ and we managed to get on.

We arrived at the port and soon we were ⁸_____ the ferry and on our way to Elba. I was really pleased that I was ⁹_____ at last and could have a ¹⁰_____ time for a couple of weeks, but it would have been even better if we didn't have the stressful start to our holiday!

Grammar 2 past perfect simple; past perfect continuous

1 Complete the sentences with the past perfect simple form of the verbs.

1 When I got to the shops, I realised I _____ (leave) my money at home.

2 By the time we got to the house, the police _____ (arrive).

3 When I got up, my sisters _____ (go) to school.

4 I didn't know that you _____ (already / visit) Canada.

5 Why didn't you tell me you _____ (see) this film before?

6 I wasn't nervous when we took off because I _____ (fly) before.

2 Complete the sentences with the past perfect continuous form of the verbs.

1 I _____ (wait) at the bus stop for over an hour before a bus finally arrived.

2 She _____ (work) as a tour operator for five years before she left.

3 We _____ (not / play) for long when Dad arrived and we had to leave.

4 How long _____ (you / look) for a holiday home before you found this one?

5 The chairs were wet because it _____ (rain) for several hours.

6 The cabin looked great because they _____ (clean) it all morning.

3 Complete the second sentence so that it has a similar meaning to the first.

1 Simon started walking at six o'clock.

By nine o'clock, Simon _____ for three hours.

2 Susan ran for twenty minutes and she got tired.

Susan got tired because she _____ for twenty minutes.

3 They had lunch at one o'clock. The trip began at two o'clock.

They _____ lunch before the trip began.

4 First, Jill packed her bag. Then she called for a taxi.

Jill _____ her bag before she called for a taxi.

5 Nat got to the river ten minutes before us and waited.

Nat _____ for ten minutes at the river before we got there.

4 Complete the blog with the correct form of the verbs in brackets.

My recent trip to Jamaica was a real experience. I called for a taxi to come at 8.30 to take us to the airport. It was late so that when it arrived, we ¹ _____ (wait) outside the house with all our baggage for nearly thirty minutes. When we arrived at the airport, I realised I ² _____ (leave) my boarding pass on the back seat of the taxi. By the time we got to the gate, they ³ _____ (start) to board the passengers. I explained my problem and they printed a new boarding pass, but not before I ⁴ _____ (pay) 50 euros.

The flight was good but, when we arrived, we got a shock. It ⁵ _____ (rain) for the previous three days and there was water everywhere. They ⁶ _____ (stop) all the traffic on the main roads, so our coach to the hotel ⁷ _____ (not / arrive) when we came out of the airport. We had to wait for several hours until they ⁸ _____ (clear) all the roads. All in all, it wasn't a very relaxing start to a holiday in a place I ⁹ _____ (always / think) was sunny every day of the year.

↻ Grammar references 7.3 and 7.4, p167–168 in Student's Book

Writing using narrative tenses; using structure; writing a story

1 Read the writing task and answer the questions.

> Your English teacher has asked you to write a story. Your story must begin with this sentence.
>
> *The teenagers were really scared and they had no idea where they were.*

1 Is someone lost? _____

2 How are they feeling? _____

3 What do you think they will do? _____

2 Read Ralf's plan for the story in Exercise 1. Then match the paragraphs (A–D) with the plan.

Story plan

1 Start with the given sentence and say where the story is set. _____

2 Describe the scene and give more details. Say why they were there. _____

3 Introduce the main character(s) and their plan of action. _____

4 Describe what happens next and how the story ends. _____

A They ran over to Rose and saw that she had fallen into a river, so they quickly pulled her out of the water. She was crying with pain. Luckily, Emilia noticed that she was able to use her phone here and she managed to call for help.

B The teenagers were really scared and they had no idea where they were. It was getting late and their phones didn't work here in the forest.

C One of the girls, Rose, said she was going to look for help. She had only been gone a few moments when suddenly the others heard a loud scream.

D The friends were on a weekend trip to celebrate the end of school. They had been exploring the forest all afternoon. But nobody had been looking at the map and now they were lost.

3 Read the Exam Reminder. In the story in Exercise 2, which paragraph gives the most information about the situation and characters?

4 Read and complete the Exam Task below Don't forget to use the Useful Language on page 87 of your Student's Book.

Exam TASK

Writing a story

Your English teacher has asked you to write a story. Your story must begin with this sentence.

They were walking down to the beach when they heard a strange noise behind them.

Write your answer in about **100 words**.

Reading
checking the information; multiple choice with five short texts

1 Read the Exam Reminder. What do you need to think about when you first read the text?

_____

2 Read and complete the Exam Task.

Exam TASK

Multiple choice with five short texts

For each question, choose the correct answer A, B or C.

1

Ice Sculptors' Club Open Evening

Have you ever wanted to be a sculptor? Join us and see what you can make from a giant block of ice. We'll provide all the equipment, but wear some warm clothes. **Beginners welcome.**

A You have to bring special tools to make the sculptures.
B It may be cold when you're there.
C It's not suitable for someone trying it for the first time.

2

Evening Drama Class

Have you ever thought about learning how to act? After a few classes, many people find they love being on the stage and say it also makes them more confident in social situations. It doesn't matter if you have no experience and it's easy to join in after school or work. Young and old welcome. Interested? We're in the main theatre, so come and have a chat.

The Drama Team

A The acting course is only for adults.
B The course may help you with other life skills.
C You need to have acted before to take part.

3

Weekend squash tournament 9th–10th May

This year's event should be more challenging than ever because we've invited two other schools to join in.

Games start at 11 a.m. each day and should be finished by 4 p.m. There will be prizes on the final day.

Entry price €5.

A Students have to pay to play in the tournament.
B The tournament is for students from one school.
C The matches will be in the evening.

4

Hi Martha

I found this online. What do you think? I could do it before we start to set up the website. Then I could share with you what I learned. Let's chat about it.

Fran

2-day online course in graphic design

Learn the basics of graphic design with this short course. We'll show you how to use photos, create different types of text and make awesome online content. Free downloads of basic programme provided. You just need your laptop and a good internet connection, as well as good general computer skills.

A Martha wants Fran to do an online course with her.
B People on the course have to pay for the software they use.
C Fran would learn some useful website skills to share with Martha.

5

School rules
1. No eating or drinking in the school building.
2. Use of mobile phones not permitted in lessons.
3. School uniform to be worn at all times except for sports activities.
4. Students need written permission to leave school before the end of lessons at 4 p.m.

A You need a letter if you want to go home early.
B You have to wear school uniform for every activity at school.
C You can't take your mobile into school.

Vocabulary 1 free-time activities; verbs of opinion

1 Complete the sentences with these words.

> backpacking   cooking   drama
> graphic design   sailing   sculpture
> squash   using social media

1 I've always liked drawing and _____ is my favourite subject at college.

2 My friend is good at acting and she does _____ lessons in her free time.

3 I'm trying to improve my _____ skills and I'm really pleased with some of the dishes I've made.

4 _____ is fun, but you need to carefully choose which sites you go on.

5 I think _____ is a great way to spend your free time. Last week I made a 3D model of a tree.

6 _____ is a great game. The only problem is that you always have to play it indoors.

7 I've tried _____ with friends, but I'm not very confident in water, so I prefer not to go too often.

8 In my opinion, _____ is perfect for young people because it lets you travel around cheaply.

2 Complete the sentences with these words.

> computer   life jacket   paintbrush
> smartphone   tent   trainers

1 When you go camping in wet conditions you need a really good _____ to keep the water out.

2 I love my _____ because they're comfortable when I wear them all day.

3 It's important to wear a _____ when you go sailing.

4 To get that effect, an artist needs a special type of _____ .

5 Nowadays, people look at their _____ over 100 times a day.

6 Very few people had a personal _____ until the 1990s. The first ones were very slow too.

3 Choose the correct option to complete the sentences.

1 My friend *makes / reads* video clips to upload.

2 I like to *play / do* music when I'm studying.

3 Andy would love to *make / write* poetry as a job.

4 I *perform / play* computer games in my free time.

5 She *listens / goes* to podcasts on her phone.

6 Do you ever *watch / listen to* ballet on TV?

7 I *photograph / make* wildlife when I'm on holiday.

8 I often *go to / watch* sports on TV on Saturday afternoons.

4 Complete the sentences with these words.

adore	can't	hate	lot	quite	would

1 I _____ stand fish. It's horrible.

2 I _____ like this song, but it's not my favourite.

3 They _____ football and never watch it.

4 She likes pasta a _____ and eats it every day.

5 I _____ this music. I could listen to it all day.

6 My mum _____ love to visit Venice one day.

Grammar 1 modals and semi-modals (1)

1 Are these sentences about ability (A), advice and suggestions (AS) or possibility and certainty (PC).

1 You must be thirsty after all that running. _____
2 You should use a different paintbrush. _____
3 I remember his brother could swim well. _____
4 They ought to speak to their teacher. _____
5 We were able to get to the concert. _____
6 That can't be right. _____
7 They shouldn't take photos here. _____
8 Ivan may be able to join us later. _____

2 Choose the correct option to complete the sentences.

1 That *can / may* be Pete's number, but let me just check.
2 You *should / may* get them a present. They've been really kind to us.
3 You *mustn't / weren't able* copy during the test.
4 I tried all morning, but I *could / wasn't able to* speak to anyone about it.
5 That *mustn't / must* be them. They always arrive at this time.
6 You *can / can't* be serious about that.
7 You *ought to / are able* speak to your parents about it.
8 You *aren't able / can't* wear those shoes on the court.

3 Which sentence, a or b, is the most similar in meaning to the original sentence?

1 I think it's a good idea for you to study a bit more.
   a You ought to study a bit more.
   b You are able to study a bit more.
2 Sorry, it's not possible for you to enter that room.
   a You might not enter that room.
   b You can't enter that room.
3 I'm certain they're out because the lights are off.
   a They can be out because the lights are off.
   b They must be out because the lights are off.
4 It wasn't possible to visit Jenny in hospital.
   a We shouldn't visit Jenny in hospital.
   b We couldn't visit Jenny in hospital.

Listening predicting what you will hear; multiple choice with picture options

1 Read the Exam Reminder. What should you do when you look at the pictures?

_____

2 **8.1 ▶** Listen and complete the Exam Task.

Exam TASK

Multiple choice with picture options
For each question, choose the correct answer.

1 What hobby has Salwa taken up?

A   B   C

2 Which activity does Matt find the most enjoyable?

A   B   C

3 Where is Kat's gym bag?

A   B   C

4 What activity is Dan probably going to take up?

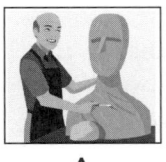  

A   B   C

5 What does Adam need to have for the activity?

A   B   C

↻ Grammar reference 8.1, p168 in Student's Book

Vocabulary 2 phrasal verbs (2); adjectives

1 Choose the correct option to complete the sentences.

1 Do you want to *join in / get together* and watch a film later?

2 I'd love to *take up / set up* skateboarding as a hobby.

3 We're going to play beach volleyball. Would you like to *join in / take up*?

4 I'm visiting Sercan and Anna later. Why don't you *give up / come round*?

5 We *gave up / set up* a group to improve public transport for young people in our area.

6 I never *hang out / come round* with my friends after school.

7 I haven't got time to go to the gym, so I've decided to *give up / join in* and go walking instead.

8 I like most of my classmates, but there are two that I don't *get together / get along with*.

2 Choose the correct option to complete the sentences.

1 That lasagna was *awesome / frightening*. Can we have it again next week?

2 The play was *enjoyable / awful*, so we left twenty minutes before the end.

3 That film was so *amazing / scary*. I couldn't even look at the screen most of the time.

4 I don't like the new restaurant because the food is really *pleasant / strange*.

5 We had a(n) *challenging / amazing* time on holiday. We didn't want to come home.

6 The bike accident I had was really *awesome / frightening*. Now I don't want to cycle any more.

7 We had a really *pleasant / strange* day at the beach because it was lovely and warm.

8 The course was *challenging / frightening* because we had to get up at 5 a.m.

9 The shopping mall was *pleasant / crazy* today. There were long queues everywhere.

10 The walk was very relaxing and I found it more *enjoyable / strange* than I'd imagined.

3 Complete the text with these words and expressions.

> amazing   challenging   crazy   enjoyable
> get along with   get together   give up
> hang out   join in   scary   set up
> take up

They [1] _____ a drama club at my local school last month and I decided to [2] _____ acting as my new hobby. My parents get home from work late and I hate staying at home by myself, but this way I can also [3] _____ with my schoolmates before the club starts. That's one of the reasons why I decided to [4] _____ .

Some of the other people in the group are [5] _____ actors and I [6] _____ them very well.

I found it hard to act at first and after the first session I wanted to [7] _____ . But friends told me to try again and now I find it really [8] _____ .

We've been preparing an end-of-term play which we'll perform on Saturday. I think it'll be a bit [9] _____ to get up in front of two hundred people, but the others told me not to worry. It can be really [10] _____ to remember everything you have to say when you are up on stage. I imagine that must be quite hard for professional actors too. Everybody's going a bit [11] _____ at the moment as there are lots of things to finish before the play. Everybody is going to [12] _____ and have a party after the show and I'm really looking forward to it.

Grammar 2 modals and semi-modals (2); expanding your vocabulary; open cloze

1 **What do these sentences show? Match them with the headings. Write A, B or C.**

> A lack of obligation or necessity
> B necessity, obligation and prohibition
> C permission and requests

1 You don't have to translate every word. Just try to understand the general meaning. _____

2 You mustn't be late. _____

3 We don't need to buy any food because we've got plenty in the fridge. _____

4 You can go home early from work if you want. _____

5 Could you send me a copy of my booking, please? _____

6 I must call my aunt this weekend. _____

7 We have to wear uniform at our school. _____

8 You can help yourself to anything you like to eat. _____

9 Can I have a quick look at your newspaper? _____

10 We don't need to get together to discuss this. _____

2 **Complete the text with these words.**

> can   have   mustn't   needn't   ought to

The Empire run-up

Some people have very unusual hobbies. In New York, USA, you can sometimes see people running up the stairs inside the Empire State Building! It's an annual race which you ¹ _____ only take part in if you are invited. You ² _____ be a professional athlete because the race is only open to people who enjoy running as a hobby.

The competitors ³ _____ to meet at the entrance and then run up the stairs, all the way to the top of this famous building. They ⁴ _____ buy special shoes for the event as they can use their regular trainers. However, competitors ⁵ _____ train as much as possible before the event because it's really challenging.

3 **Read the Exam Reminder. Then complete the Exam Task.**

Exam TASK

Open cloze

For each question, write the correct answer. Write **one** word for each gap.

I want to tell you all about a new sport I've taken ¹ _____ recently. It's called freerunning. Freerunning means running, jumping and climbing from one space to another. You ² _____ do it anywhere you like, but it's great in the city centre. You don't ³ _____ any special equipment, but you ⁴ _____ to be quite fit.

Anybody can join ⁵ _____ and it's a great way to hang ⁶ _____ with your friends and get some exercise at the same time.

↻ Grammar reference 8.1, p168 in Student's Book

Writing linking words and phrases (1); adding details; writing an article

1 Choose the correct linking word.

1 It's a really challenging activity, but it's enjoyable *too / also*.

2 I spend too much time on social media sites *such / like* Facebook and Instagram.

3 You only need a few things to start painting. *For instance / Like*, a good paintbrush is really important.

4 *Such / As* the weather was so bad, we decided not to play tennis and went home instead.

5 My aunt photographs wildlife in places *such as / for example* New Zealand and Australia.

6 I often watch ballet on TV *such as / since* my partner loves it.

2 Look at the writing task and answer the questions.

> You see this notice on your school website.
> 1 What sport / activity does your brother, sister, friend or cousin do?
> 2 Why do they like this sport / activity?
> 3 Would you like to try it?
>
> Write an article answering these questions and we will put it on our website.
>
> Write your article in about **100 words**.

1 Do you have to write about a sport or activity that you do? _____

2 How many different questions do you have to answer? _____

3 Read a student's answer to the task in Exercise 2. Complete the sentences with linking words from the Learning Reminder. More than one answer may be correct.

> My sister loves playing squash. She's part of a local team and plays for our school ¹ _____ . She trains a couple of times a week and has matches at the weekend ² _____ .
>
> I think she enjoys it ³ _____ she can play it all year round as it's played indoors. She says it's an awesome feeling when you beat someone.
>
> I definitely wouldn't like to play squash. The players are a bit boring. ⁴ _____ , when they go out, they only talk about squash. I also prefer being in the open air and doing something ⁵ _____ jogging or running.

4 Read the Exam Reminder. What do you need to do in the first sentence of each paragraph?

_____

5 Read and complete the Exam Task. Don't forget to use the Useful Language on page 99 of your Student's Book.

Exam TASK

Writing an article

You see this advert on an English-language website.

> **Articles wanted**
>
> **Your own time**
> 1 What's your favourite activity / sport to do with your friends?
> 2 What's your favourite activity / sport to do on your own?
> 3 How often do you do each activity and why do you enjoy it?

Write an article answering these questions for our website.

Write your article in about **100 words**.

Reading
identifying topics; matching sentences to gaps

1 Read the Exam Reminder. What words do you need to look for before or after the gap in the text?

Identifying topics

- Read the whole text for general meaning before you look at the sentences.
- Look for the topic of each paragraph. Then look at sentences A–H to see which topic in the text they match.
- Read the text again and look for key words before and after the gap. Look for nouns and pronouns which will give you clues, e.g. *this, these, it, them*. For example, the sentence in lines 7 and 8, has two pronouns (*these* and *ones*) that refer to shops. *These clearly want to know you just as well as the online ones*. Pay attention also to linking words like *for example* or time words such as *first of all* and *then*.
- When you have chosen your sentence, read the complete text again together with the sentences you have matched. Make sure the sentences fit well with the rest of the text.

2 Read and complete the Exam Task.

Exam **TASK**

Matching sentences to gaps

Five sentences have been removed from the text. For each question, choose the correct answer. There are three extra sentences which you do not need to use.

A After that, you are likely to receive messages the following Mondays for stores in and around the airport.

B As a result, you never know if you are being watched.

C Many shoppers will be annoyed by these, but some are happy to receive offers and discounts directly on their phone.

D Once the app has been downloaded, it tracks your precise position using several different satellites.

E There are several things you can do to stop shops from following your movements.

F For example, they are familiar with which pages you have visited and probably your age and interests too.

G This is a problem because the seller wants to know exactly what part of the store interests you the most.

H Airports can be very busy places at the weekends.

Every step you take

1   When you buy something online, the seller already knows a lot about you. **(1)** _____ They will also know what model of computer or phone you are using and this may mean that you are offered a higher or lower price for the same product.

Online shops clearly have an advantage then. However, most people (75%) still buy from traditional shops. These clearly want to know you just as well as the online ones do. You usually start giving them information when
10   you download a shop's app or sign up for one of their cards. But that's just the start. **(2)** _____ As you are now being followed, a shop knows if you are close by and you may be sent an 'interesting offer' or 'special promotion'. As with buying online, these offers are carefully based on what you have bought before or products you have asked about.

Of course, these apps can be deleted, but your information may still be sold to other companies. These will then use it to send you their own offers for things they think you'd
20   like to buy. That's why some shoppers receive lots of messages every time they go near the town or city centre.

(3) _____ The secret is not to send so many messages that the customer cancels or switches off the app.

Satellite technologies tell sellers exactly where you are in the city, but the satellites can't see exactly where you are inside their shop. **(4)** _____ The solution is to put special devices inside the shop. These will connect with your phone and tell the shop your exact in-store location. For example, if you are walking through
30   the clothes department, you will receive details of special offers on the new collection. If you move to the electronics department, you'll receive offers for gadgets and other devices.

Your daily habits are also known to a lot of people. If you have been at the airport for the last three Mondays, this information will be collected and shared. **(5)** _____ And it doesn't matter if in the future you stop flying on that day. The sellers already know that you are a regular plane traveller and probably
40   have money to spend on high-level products. So, think carefully before you sign up for that attractive store app.

Vocabulary 1 computers and technology

1 Choose the correct option to complete the sentences.

1 I've bought a new *equipment / smartphone* because my old one was broken.

2 I think WiFi was a really good *software / invention*.

3 We need to buy new *server / hardware* for our computer system every two or three years.

4 You'll need to change your *webcam / software* for our next conference call – I can hardly see your face.

5 How did people use a computer without a *software / mouse* to move around the screen?

6 I'm sorry, but we can't send or receive messages today because the *webcam / server* is down.

7 The computer itself wasn't expensive, but I spent a lot on all the *software / server* I needed.

8 I love computer games, but you need lots of expensive extra *invention / equipment* to make them work.

2 Complete the text with the correct form of these words.

crash	create	design	develop
equipment	install	instructions	test

I heard they had ¹ _____ a great new computer game, so I bought it. I've managed to ² _____ it on my computer but unfortunately it ³ _____ every time I try to open it. I'm so annoyed. And I don't think they've ⁴ _____ this game very well. First, you need some really expensive ⁵ _____ to run it and secondly the ⁶ _____ are impossible to understand. I think they probably ⁷ _____ the game in a hurry and didn't ⁸ _____ it properly.

3 Complete the comments with the correct form of these words.

change	connection	experiment
install	instructions	internet	invention
lab	server	webcam

The ¹ _____ is a wonderful ² _____ that ³ _____ many people's lives. But in my apartment block we have a really bad ⁴ _____ , so we can't really enjoy it.

The newspapers were full of news about a young scientist who did an amazing ⁵ _____ in a local ⁶ _____ .

There's a huge room on the ground floor which is full of the office ⁷ _____ .

Where can I buy a new ⁸ _____ ? I just found out that my computer hasn't got one and I need to make some video calls.

Why do they make it so difficult to ⁹ _____ new software? It should be really easy, but sometimes the ¹⁰ _____ are really complicated

Grammar 1 the passive (1); passive sentences with modals; *by* and *with*

1 Complete the sentences with the passive form of the verb.

1 This software _____ (can / download) directly from our website.

2 Your machine _____ (will / test) in our lab over the next few days.

3 The instructions _____ (must / read) very carefully before you start.

4 All the software _____ (just / install) on your computer, so it's ready to use now.

5 Special equipment _____ (use) to do last month's test.

6 Your new mouse _____ (will / send) to your home address in the next few days.

2 Write complete sentences with the passive form of the verb and *by* or *with*.

1 This software / develop / our competitor / a few years ago.

_____

_____

2 Your computer screen / must clean / a special liquid.

_____

_____

3 Your computer /should check / one of our engineers.

_____

_____

4 My mouse / damage / my son / yesterday.

_____

_____

5 I / show around / the offices this morning / one of my new colleagues.

_____

_____

6 The door / can only open / a special key.

_____

_____

3 Change the sentences from active to passive.

1 We tested the new product in the laboratory.
The new product _____ .

2 A friend of mine broke my webcam.
My webcam _____ .

3 One of our staff will repair your computer.
Your computer _____ .

4 Users must read the instructions before starting.
The instructions _____ .

Listening listening again; multiple choice with one conversation

1 Read the Exam Reminder. What should you do when you hear the recording the first time?

_____

2 9.1 ▶ Listen and complete the Exam Task.

Exam TASK

Multiple choice with one conversation

For each question, choose the correct answer. You will hear an interview with a woman called Emma, who is a social media communications expert.

1 According to Emma, the biggest mistake people make on social media is
  A making their personal data public.
  B talking about their holidays.
  C uploading pictures of themselves and friends.

2 When you upload photos on social media
  A they may contain data about where you are.
  B people won't know where you really are.
  C people know you're not working or studying.

3 Young people often give away personal details by uploading photos of
  A their holidays.
  B their 16th birthday party.
  C a personal document.

4 According to Emma, doing a quiz on social media
  A involves lots of useless information.
  B could help someone get your passwords.
  C helps people to understand your habits.

5 At the end, Emma says that
  A we are now more protected online.
  B people meet each other more often online than in person these days.
  C we tell people more about ourselves on social media than in person.

◀ ⟳ **Grammar references 9.1, 9.2 and 9.3, p169 in Student's Book**

Vocabulary 2 technology verbs; prepositions (2)

1 Choose the correct option to complete the sentences.

1 I *deleted / dragged* some important files by mistake.

2 If you don't want that image any more just *click / switch* the 'delete' button.

3 I've *signed up / connected* for a new online TV channel that shows my favourite sitcoms.

4 Don't *upload / download* files if you don't know what they are.

5 You can simply *drag / connect* the picture to another part of the screen.

6 I've been trying to *download / connect* to the internet all morning.

7 When you've finished, you can *switch / upload* your files to the server.

8 I *chatted / signed up* with other people online.

9 A lot of people forget to *click / switch* off their computer when they have finished using it.

2 Complete the sentences with the correct form of a verb from Exercise 1 and a preposition.

1 Oh no! I can't _____ the internet now and I've got an online lesson in a few minutes.

2 I think I've _____ some important files _____ my computer. I can't find them anywhere!

3 If I were you, I'd _____ their newsletter. It's got some interesting articles in it.

4 I love _____ people in other countries who share my interests.

5 You need to _____ the file name twice to open it.

6 Please remember to _____ your laptop before you go to bed.

7 I really like that video we made of the school concert. I'm going to _____ it _____ my personal page.

8 They _____ the band's new song _____ the official site yesterday.

9 If you want to save time, just _____ the image directly _____ your desktop.

3 Choose the correct option to complete the sentences.

1 We carried *in / out* the changes you asked for.

2 I'd love to be an expert *in / for* computers, but I don't understand them at all.

3 My team has been trying for years, but this time we succeeded *in / on* winning the league.

4 We're still looking *for / about* answers to the problem with the server.

5 I bought a DVD of the film instead *for / of* downloading it.

6 It's easy to communicate *to / with* friends online if you have the right equipment.

4 Complete the sentences with the correct word or phrase from Exercise 3.

1 **A:** What are you _____ ?
   B: My mouse. Have you seen it?

2 My sister's a(n) _____ business software.

3 I don't know how but we _____ beating the other team.

4 They _____ all the work in just two days.

5 We decided to stay at home _____ going out.

6 As the captain, you need to _____ everybody in your team.

Grammar 2 the passive (2)

1 Choose the correct option to complete the sentences.

1 Sorry I can't send it from that computer. It *is being used / is used* by somebody else.

2 Oh no! My smartphone *is stolen / has been stolen*.

3 I was happy when I got home because my laptop *was being / had been* repaired and I could use it again.

4 I made a sandwich while the file *has been / was being* downloaded.

5 When I got back to my hotel room, I noticed that it *hadn't been / wasn't* cleaned.

6 Your pictures *are being / were* printed at the moment.

7 Are you sure the test *has been / has* cancelled?

8 They told me I couldn't use my computer because the new software *was / was being* installed.

2 Complete the sentences with the passive form of the verbs in brackets.

1 I can't wear my favourite shirt because it _____ (wash) at the moment.

2 I couldn't download anything from the site this morning because it _____ (update).

3 I hear the old church _____ (turn into) a new restaurant. Is it any good?

4 I had a shock when I came out of the shop because my bike _____ (steal) while I was inside.

5 The hotel was in a mess when we arrived because it _____ (paint) and the workers hadn't finished.

6 Oh no! All my photos _____ (delete) by a virus. I can't find any of them.

3 Complete the passive sentences so they have the same meaning as the active one.

1 We've followed all the instructions.
   All the instructions _____ .

2 They're filling the swimming pool with water.
   The swimming pool _____ with water.

3 When I came back from holiday, they'd completed all the work.
   When I came back from holiday, all the work _____ .

4 They're checking everybody's passport.
   Everybody's passport _____ .

5 We have sent all the documents by post.
   All the documents _____ by post.

6 I can't use the car this evening because they're repairing it.
   I can't use the car this evening because it _____ .

4 Complete the blog with the correct form of the verbs in brackets.

Has your computer [1] _____ (ever / attack)? Mine has and right now it [2] _____ (repair) because the other evening someone stole all my files! I was working late at night when I realised that my files and programs [3] _____ (delete) one by one, right in front of my eyes. I tried to switch off the PC, but it seemed that the computer and mouse [4] _____ (operate) by somebody else, so I couldn't do anything. When I tried to re-start the computer, I just got a blank screen. I called my local computer shop the next day. They told me that a lot of computers [5] _____ (attack) this way in the previous weeks. They also told me that a couple of people [6] _____ (arrest) by the police earlier that day. Talking to friends, I've learned that lots of computers [7] _____ (damage) like this recently. It's also really annoying that so little [8] _____ (do) at the moment to stop this.

Grammar reference 9.4, p169 in Student's Book

Writing
presenting your ideas in order; writing about your opinion; writing an opinion essay

1 **Read the writing task and the Exam Reminder. Then answer the questions.**

Some people think that new digital technology makes people's lives more difficult instead of making them easier. What's your opinion?

1 Do you need to talk about facts or what you think about something?

_____

2 What do you need to do before you start writing?

_____

2 **Read a student's answer to the task in Exercise 1. Number the paragraphs in order. Write 1–5.**

A Lastly, I believe people have forgotten how much harder life without mobile communications was, especially in emergency situations. _____

B Firstly, people forget that new digital technology helps with our everyday school or working lives. If we have to write an essay, it's easy to find the information on the internet. Before, students had to go to the library or ask their parents. _____

C In conclusion, I really think that technology makes our lives easier because we can do so many things just by clicking on something. _____

D Most people like new digital technology and the way their lives have been changed by it, but others don't. In my opinion, technology has made our lives much easier. _____

E Furthermore, people forget that technology makes many other things simpler. With smartphones, we can look at maps when we're lost, for example. _____

3 **Underline the linking words used in the opinion essay in Exercise 2.**

4 **Read the Exam Reminder again. What *shouldn't* you use in an opinion essay?**

_____

5 **Look again at the student's answer in Exercise 2. Which point in the Exam Reminder did the student *not* follow?**

_____

6 **Read and complete the Exam Task. Don't forget to use the Useful Language on page 111 of your Student's Book.**

Exam **TASK**

Writing an opinion essay
Some people think that the internet makes students lazy because they can just copy all the information they need from websites. What's your opinion?

Write your answer in about **100 words.**

Reading understanding key information; multiple choice with five short texts

1 **Read the Exam Reminder. How many times should you read the answer options?**

_____

2 **Read and complete the Exam Task.**

Exam TASK

Multiple choice with five short texts

For each question, choose the correct answer.

1
Last episode in the current series of the hit soap opera, Hillside. Find out what happens when Helen finally gets to meet her ex-boyfriend's new partner.
Watch at 7.30 p.m. on TV1 or available to view on channel website www.tv1catchup.com from midnight. New series returns after the summer.

The programme

A isn't going to be available online.

B will be on at the same time the following week.

C has been very popular.

2
From: info@musicfirst.com
To: federika@klippelmail.com
Subject: Enquiry
Date: 06.10

Dear Federika,
Thanks for your enquiry of 5th October about singing lessons at the end of this month. Unfortunately, we have had to put off all our new courses until the new year because of building work at our school, which should finish in mid-December.
I have attached an application form in case you are interested in starting then. If so, could you please let us have the completed form by the end of the month.
Monique Bataillard.

When does Federika need to apply for her lessons?

A By 31st December.

B At the end of October.

C 5th October.

3
FOR SALE: Grand piano

Generally good condition, just a few marks here and there.

Purchased five years ago but rarely used.

Not suitable for under 5s. Buyer to collect.

Contact me on:
0205 6497407

The advert says the piano

A is not in very good condition.

B would be good for very young children.

C will not be delivered by the seller.

4
We're looking for future stars to take part in a brand-new talent show on Channel 5. Think you've got what it takes? Come and find out. On Saturday 12th December we'll be choosing five people to appear on the show next February.

The talent show programme

A is in its second series.

B will be shown on television in February.

C will choose the best person from five candidates in December.

5
We'll pick you up from school and look for a new guitar for your lessons. Wait for us outside the school gate.
Mum and Dad

The girl's parents want to

A buy her a guitar.

B take her to a guitar lesson.

C take her to school.

Vocabulary 1 film and TV

1 Match the descriptions with these words.

| chat show | documentary | drama | horror |
| quiz show | soap opera | talent show | thriller |

1 This is a programme which tests a person's knowledge of different subjects. _____

2 This is a film that is really scary and some parts of it might be difficult to watch at times. _____

3 This is a programme which discusses a subject or topic using lots of facts and interviews. _____

4 This is a film or TV programme often about people trying to deal with difficult personal situations. _____

5 This is a TV programme where well-known people answer questions about their lives. _____

6 This programme has performances by unknown people who would like to become famous. _____

7 This is a programme which is on several times a week and follows the everyday lives of different people. _____

8 This is a film or TV programme where there is a mystery that is usually solved at the end. _____

2 Complete the sentences with these words.

| celebrity | channel | presenter | programme |
| scene | series |

1 It's my favourite _____ because it shows all the best soap operas.

2 I wouldn't like to be a news _____ . You're always telling people about bad things.

3 I'll never forget the first _____ in that horror film. It's five minutes long and really frightening.

4 I don't like that chat show because they never have a really famous _____ on it.

5 They're going to run a new _____ of my favourite quiz show in the winter.

6 I think the news is the only _____ that I watch these days.

3 Complete the conversation with the correct form of words from Exercises 1 and 2.

A: Hello. I'm doing some research on young people's TV habits. Can I ask you a few questions?

B: Sure, go ahead.

A: OK. What kind of [1] _____ do you watch?

B: Well, soap operas and dramas usually.

A: Do you ever watch [2] _____ ?

B: No, I hate listening to people talking about what they've done all their life. I never watch those.

A: And what about [3] _____ ?

B: No. I always get the answers wrong!

A: Do you have a favourite [4] _____ ?

B: I think it must be ABC2 because it has good films and awesome [5] _____ about the environment.

Grammar 1
reported speech: statements; changes to pronouns, possessives, time and place

1 Read the direct speech sentences. Then complete the reported speech sentences.

1 'I'm taking the last train' she said.
She said _____ .

2 'I saw some good paintings at the exhibition'.
She said _____ .

3 'You can go to the party.'
Nell said _____ .

4 'Your brother must learn an instrument to join the band'.
She said _____ .

5 'We'll come round later'.
They said _____ .

6 'You haven't visited us recently'.
They said _____ .

7 'We'll arrive a bit late tomorrow morning'.
They said _____ .

8 'I spoke to my cousin last night'.
She said _____ .

9 'I called your mobile about an hour ago'.
Kevin said _____ .

10 'I couldn't watch the film yesterday.'
Linda said _____ .

11 'We aren't coming to your birthday party next week'.
They said _____ .

12 'We'll meet you outside the cinema this afternoon'.
They said _____ .

2 Write the words Antoine and Marta actually said.

1 Antoine told Marta he hadn't seen her for a while.
_____

2 Marta said she had been busy with her family for the last few days.
_____

3 Antoine told her there was a good horror film on TV that evening. He said she was welcome to come round and see it with him.
_____

4 She said she had seen one a few weeks before and never wanted to see one again.
_____

5 She said she was going home then but she would be in touch the day after.
_____

Listening
completing information; gap fill

1 Read the Exam Reminder. What do you need to do when you look at the heading and the information?

_____

2 10.1▶ Listen and complete the Exam Task.

Exam TASK

Gap fill

For each question, write the correct answer in the gap. Write one or two words or a number or a date or a time.

You will hear a presenter talking about a music festival.

The NorthSide Music Festival

The festival is a three-day event held in early
1 _____ .

The first event was in June 2010 with five groups from Denmark.

Last year over 2 _____ people attended.

Concert held in Aarhus which is Denmark's
3 _____ .

Festival promotes 4 _____ Indie bands.

Aims of the concert: to offer great music and be the 5 _____ festival in that region.

Event will remain small, so it can stay in the
6 _____ .

↻ Grammar references 10.1 and 10.2, p169–170 in Student's Book

Vocabulary 2 phrasal verbs (3); predicting possible answers; multiple-choice cloze

1 **Choose the correct option to complete the sentences.**

1 The old concert hall has been turned *into / out* a multi-screen cinema.

2 Can you turn *out / up* the volume? I can't hear well.

3 The chat show was really boring, so I turned it *off / up* and went to bed.

4 We tried to set up an online concert site, but it didn't turn *up / out* very well.

5 We were playing our favourite music loudly in the garden, but our neighbour asked us to turn it *up / down*.

6 There are so many buttons on this remote control. All I want to do is to turn *on / off* the TV and watch my favourite soap opera.

2 **Choose the correct option to complete the sentences.**

1 We arrived after the hotel reception had closed and ended *out / up* sleeping in the car.

2 I need to get *on / up* with my homework now.

3 We wanted to buy a few more things, but we ran *out / on* of time.

4 They put *out / off* the music festival until next weekend because of the bad weather.

5 You're home late. The match will be *out / over* in a few minutes!

6 My brother's really *into / in* heavy metal bands, but I don't like that sort of music.

3 **Complete the sentences with the correct form of these phrasal verbs.**

be into	be over	end up	get on with
put off	run out of		

1 We really enjoyed that series and were sad when it _____ .

2 We've got lots to do, so let's _____ things.

3 I started the test a bit slowly, so I _____ time at the end and couldn't finish.

4 My aunt _____ quiz shows. She watches at least two or three a day.

5 We left home a little later than planned and _____ having to run for the train.

6 I don't think it's a good idea to _____ the concert. The weather might be just as bad next week.

4 **Read the Exam Reminder. What can you do before looking at the options given?**

_____

Exam REMINDER

Predicting possible answers

- Sometimes you can guess the missing word before you look at the options.
- Read the text once and think of possible words for each gap.
- Look at the options and see if they are the same as your original idea. If not, is there a similar word?
- After you've chosen all the words for the gaps, go back and read the text again to make sure they fit.

5 **Read and complete the Exam Task.**

Exam TASK

Multiple-choice cloze

For each question, choose the correct answer.

Plus belle la vie is a French television
1 _____ opera. This year is the fourteenth 2 _____ of the show which follows the lives of ordinary people living in Marseilles. The programme is shown on France 3, a national TV 3 _____ , every Monday at 8.15 p.m. According to TV research, at least five million people 4 _____ their TVs to watch the programme, but it is likely that many more are 5 _____ this show because *Plus belle la vie* has gained a lot of fans over the years. People did not seem to like it at first and it only 6 _____ out to be a big success in its second year.

1 **A** soap **B** show **C** television **D** gossip
2 **A** number **B** talent **C** series **D** quiz
3 **A** series **B** channel **C** programme **D** show
4 **A** turn off **B** turn out **C** turn into **D** turn on
5 **A** fan **B** up **C** into **D** on
6 **A** turned **B** made **C** put **D** showed

Grammar 2 reported speech: questions and requests

1 **Tick (✔) the sentences that are correct. Rewrite the ones that are incorrect.**

1 He asked the reporters why were they following him.

_____

2 I asked where did they come from.

_____

3 Barnie asked if we were going to watch the quiz show that evening.

_____

4 My brother asked if he could borrow my scarf.

_____

5 Mum asked if I already finish my homework.

_____

6 She asked what did I want to drink.

_____

2 **Change the direct speech into reported speech.**

1 'Can you turn the music down?' she asked me.

She asked me _____

_____ .

2 'What channel is the film on?' asked Tim.

Tim asked me _____

_____ .

3 'How did the show turn out?' Mum asked.

Mum asked us _____

_____ .

4 'Do we have to watch this terrible soap opera?' Ben asked.

Ben asked _____

_____ .

3 **Rewrite the reported speech as direct speech.**

1 Ruth asked me if I had time for a coffee.

_____

asked Ruth.

2 Harry asked Emily if she would turn down the music.

_____

asked Harry.

3 My parents asked why I had done so badly in the test the day before.

_____

asked my parents.

4 My best friend asked me if she could borrow my bike.

_____

asked my best friend.

4 **Read the conversation. Then complete the reported speech below.**

Leo: Hi Anita. How are you?

Anita: Hi Leo. I'm fine, thanks. I've just finished watching my favourite chat show and now I'm going out with some friends.

Leo: Where are you going?

Anita: Into town. Do you want to join us?

Leo: I can't. I've got lots of homework to do! Actually, if you've got a moment, can you help me with my English exercises?

Anita: Sorry Leo, I haven't got time. But we'll have a look together tomorrow morning before lessons start.

Leo asked Anita [1] _____ and she said that [2] _____ fine and that she [3] _____ watching her favourite chat show. She also said she [4] _____ with some friends and asked Leo if he [5] _____ to join them. Leo said he [6] _____ because he [7] _____ lots of homework to do. He then asked Anita if she [8] _____ help him with his English homework. Anita told Leo she was sorry, but she [9] _____ time. She said they [10] _____ a look together before lessons the following morning.

⟳ Grammar reference 10.3, p170 in Student's Book

Writing
showing the order of events; checking your story; writing a story

Learning **REMINDER**

Showing the order of events

- Remember that there are words and phrases to help you order your ideas when you write a story.
- Introduce the first action with *First of all*, e.g. *First of all, the actress came into the studio.*
- For two actions happening at the same time, use *while*, e.g. *The audience listened carefully while the actress spoke.*
- For actions that happen one after another, use *then, after that, after* or *before*, e.g. *Before the interview had finished, the actress got very angry with the presenter for one of his questions. Then she refused to answer any more questions.*
- Introduce the last event with *Finally* or *In the end*, e.g. *Finally, the actress got up and walked out of the studio.*

1 Complete the sentences with these words.

after	before	finally	first	then	while

1 We sat for more than three hours watching the play. _____ , we got up, left the theatre and went home.

2 He was watching a soap opera _____ his partner was reading a newspaper.

3 _____ going to the cinema, they had dinner in a restaurant. There was no time to eat after the film.

4 First, the presenter forgot the name of the guest. _____ that, the sound didn't work and we couldn't hear what she was saying.

5 We are driving to the airport. _____ we are catching a plane to Mallorca.

6 _____ of all, the presenter introduced the actors to the audience.

2 Read the writing task and circle the correct options.

Your English teacher has asked you to write a story. Your story must begin with this sentence.

I felt so nervous when the quiz show presenter introduced me to the audience.

1 You need to write a *letter / story*.

2 You need to write about something that happened to *you / another person*.

3 Now read a student's answer to the task in Exercise 2. Complete the sentences with the words from Exercise 1.

I felt so nervous when the quiz show presenter introduced me to the audience. [1] _____ of all, he asked me how I was feeling and I said I was OK.

[2] _____ the presenter started the quiz by asking me questions on geography. For example, he asked me which continent the Sahara was in and, luckily, I knew the answer.

[3] _____ that, he asked me about modern music. I'm into that and had no problems answering the questions.

[4] _____ , we got to the last question. If I got it right, I'd win the competition. The presenter asked me which language people spoke in Brazil. Everybody's eyes were on me [5] _____ I was thinking about the answer. I said it was Spanish. Someone in the audience laughed loudly and I knew that I wasn't going to win anything!

4 Read the Exam Reminder. What do you need to do when you've finished writing your story?

_____

Exam **REMINDER**

Checking your story

When you finish writing your story you need to read everything again to check for mistakes in:

- spelling e.g. writing *beleive* instead of *believe*.
- grammar (e.g. verb tenses) *Yesterday I have got up early* instead of *I got up.*
- punctuation (e.g. full stops, apostrophes.) *We arrived at Jeans house Then we saw …* instead of *Jean's house. Then we saw …*
- word order (e.g. in questions, in indirect speech) e.g. *I asked her what was her name* instead of *what her name was.*
- correct choice of words (e.g. prepositions, collocations) e.g. saying *We arrived to home* instead of *We arrived home.*

5 Read and complete the Exam Task. Don't forget to use the Useful Language on page 123 of your Student's Book.

Exam **TASK**

Writing a story

Your English teacher has asked you to write a story. Your story must begin with this sentence.

This was her very first trip to a music concert.

Write your story in about **100 words.**

Reading finding distractors; matching people to texts

1 Read the Exam Reminder. Why do you need to be careful of 'distractors' in this task?

Now Hiring!

A Coach sports in Ghana

1 In a village in Ghana, this 10-week work experience gives you the opportunity to improve your skills as a sports coach. You'll organise after-school sports clubs and help improve the children's fitness levels. Popular sports include football and volleyball, but you're welcome to introduce new activities. In your spare time, you can enjoy Ghanaian culture and visit local national parks and colourful markets.

B Teach music in Bolivia

If you love music and working with young people,
10 this is the perfect opportunity for you to be a volunteer music teacher. You'll teach local primary school children about music and help them improve their musical ability. You'll work with other instructors organising fun music classes and helping the children to learn.

C Environmental volunteer in Colombia

This is a six-week work experience position working in a small organisation in the centre of the capital city, Bogotá. You will need to help prepare presentations on our sustainability projects and type up reports.
20 This opportunity is just right for a young person who believes in protecting the environment. Grants available for accommodation costs.

D IT work experience in Berlin

We have a paid summer work opportunity with a small company in central Berlin for a young person with good IT skills. You'll be involved in research on ecotourism topics and creating materials for social media. You may also have the chance to work with the company's clients.

E Provide after-school care in Italy

This three-month work experience involves helping
30 children in big cities. As children often spend their afternoons on the streets, you'll work with our organisation to offer fun activities which include art, cooking, games and music. Your mornings are free to take advantage of the Italian language lessons provided. You are also free at weekends, so you'll have plenty of time to explore this beautiful country.

F Summer Camp volunteer

Have an amazing summer working at our Summer Camp in California. The only thing that matters is to have fun and make new friends. This year we have
40 positions for young people with the ability to teach art and drama and also help our regular instructors with sports activities. Enjoy 6–8 weeks with a wonderful team of hardworking young people.

G Farm work in Patagonia

We offer the chance to stay on a family-run farm. You'll need to wake up early most days. Although the work can be quite hard, it's always enjoyable. The farm is 30 km from the nearest town, so this is not the place for those who want to meet other people. You'll work for five days and then have two free days to
50 explore the incredible natural landscapes. Previous experience of farm work required.

H Pauline's Charity Shops, Melbourne, Australia

We have lots of different opportunities for young people in our charity shops. Maybe you are very creative and can make an attractive window display? Or maybe you connect easily with people and would like to work as a shop assistant? Accommodation and meals will be paid for by our organisation.

2 Read and complete the Exam Task.

Matching people to texts

The students below all want to do some work experience. Read the leaflet prepared by a school careers office with descriptions of eight possible jobs. Decide which job would be the most suitable for each student.

1  Jung is very good at communicating with people and gives piano lessons to other students after school. He also has an interest in the environment and develops his own website and blog pages. He needs to earn a little money from his work experience. _____

2  Melissa is very sociable and creative and sometimes acts in a local theatre group. She is a good football and volleyball player. She has looked after young children for her parents' friends. She can spend a maximum of two months away. _____

3  Laila loves organising activities for children. She is very keen on the environment and nature in general. She lives in the countryside and often looks after her parents' sheep and cows. She wants to be in a quiet place. _____

4  Raisa has three pets and loves animals. She works in a local shop at weekends. She is also keen on basketball and often helps her team's trainer with practice sessions. She would like to spend time in a different culture. _____

5  Greg is a very friendly person. He is really good at art and designing things, especially on the computer. He works in his parents' shop at weekends and loves meeting and helping customers. He wants to work outside Europe. _____

Vocabulary 1 education

1 Choose the correct option to complete the sentences.

1 My friend has finished university and has a *course / degree* in *economy / economics*

2 I'd like to do a yoga course, but there aren't any good *instructors / pupils* nearby.

3 I'm writing *an essay / a research* on new technology in schools.

4 I've paid a *grant / deposit* for the course and have to pay the rest next week.

5 I find *research / physics* quite difficult and it's not my favourite school subject.

6 The exam was difficult and very few *teachers / pupils* passed.

7 This course is suitable for *beginner / intermediate* students with at least two years' experience.

8 My *handwriting / application* is bad, but I can write everything on a keyboard these days.

2 Complete the sentences with these words.

beginner	certificate	diploma	fees
IT	mark	subjects	

1 I'm good with computers, so I'd like to study _____ at college.

2 I'm a _____ . I don't know anything about this sport.

3 I did a course in car mechanics and got a _____ at the end of it. The _____ is on my wall.

4 I'd like to study there, but the _____ are too high for me.

5 In the UK, students choose three or four _____ to study when they are 16.

6 I worked really hard on that essay, but my teacher still gave me a low _____ .

3 Complete the text with these words.

accent	behaves	clever	examiner
failed	passes	subject	

My brother is very ¹ _____ and has always learned things very quickly. But he's also quite a difficult student and often ² _____ badly in class. He studies as little as possible and it's amazing that he always ³ _____ his exams first time. I think he's only ⁴ _____ one in all his life and that was because he didn't like the ⁵ _____ . He wants to study French at college or university, so he'll need a good mark. I just hope the ⁶ _____ in the speaking test can understand his ⁷ _____ !

Grammar 1 the causative

1 Tick (✓) the sentences which contain a causative.

1 I've been having a problem with my computer. _____

2 Did you have your bag searched at the entrance? _____

3 I'm having the car checked because it's making a strange noise. _____

4 Have you checked the homework exercises? _____

5 Is it possible to have my copy of the book signed? _____

6 They had given away all the signed books when I arrived. _____

2 Write the words in order.

1 had / you / have / hair / your / cut / ?

_____

2 friend / having / tested / is / my / his eyes / .

_____

3 didn't / taken / photo / your / have / why / you / ?

_____

4 have / you / at the doctor's / your / checked / will / temperature / ?

_____

5 my phone / repaired / want / I / have / to / .

_____

3 Complete the sentences using the causative. Use the agent where necessary.

1 Someone is checking my computer later today.
I _____ later today.

2 A professional photographer took her photo.
She _____ .

3 Why are they cleaning your jacket?
Why are you _____ ?

4 The mechanic repaired their car.
They _____ .

5 My smartphone is being checked at the moment.
I _____ at the moment.

6 A nurse was taking the boy's temperature.
The boy _____ .

7 There wasn't time for anyone to wash the car.
We _____ because there wasn't time.

8 They're going to test my eyes tomorrow.
I _____ tomorrow.

Listening listening for feelings; multiple choice with six conversations

1 Read the Exam Reminder. Apart from the words they use, how can you understand the speaker's feelings about something?

_____

2 ▶11.1 Listen and complete the Exam Task.

Exam TASK

Multiple choice with six conversations

For each question, choose the correct answer A, B or C.

1 You will hear two friends talking about an IT course. How does the woman feel about it?
A annoyed
B happy
C disappointed

2 Why didn't the boy do the course at college?
A He didn't have the right qualifications.
B The fees were too high.
C He didn't receive a grant.

3 How did the girl feel during her survival course?
A annoyed
B embarrassed
C upset

4 How does Lindy feel about her exam result?
A She is disappointed with it.
B She is happy with it.
C She is confused by it.

5 What was the main difficulty Alice had during the spoken Italian test?
A She found the examiner's accent difficult to understand.
B The examiner found her accent difficult to understand.
C Her pronunciation wasn't clear.

6 How does Tomiko feel about her essay mark?
A upset
B anxious
C amazed

▶ Grammar reference 11.1, p171 in Student's Book

Vocabulary 2 education expressions; prepositions (3)

1 Complete the sentences with the correct form of *make, break* or *take* and one of these words.

an effort	a mistake	notes	progress
the rules	up		

1 If you _____ to do something well, you will get a good result in the end.

2 There's a lot to remember, so make sure you _____ while they're explaining everything.

3 We _____ next week and then we have two months' holiday.

4 The children are all _____ in Spanish and they can now count to a hundred.

5 You know that if you _____ , you'll get in trouble.

6 I think I _____ in my last message. We're meeting at 8 p.m., not 8.30.

2 Complete the student's blog with the correct form of the expressions from Exercise 1.

I'm enjoying my new secondary school a bit more now. I started quite badly in all subjects, but now I think I'm ¹ _____ in nearly all of them. At least that's what the teachers say. The teachers are quite strict. Last week, I ² _____ in the last question of a test and I failed the whole test – even though everything else was correct! They get very annoyed if you ³ _____ at school. For example, if you don't have the right uniform you get in a lot of trouble. That happened to me last week.

Lessons are very traditional. The teacher speaks, we listen and ⁴ _____ on the most important things. We have to ⁵ _____ to follow what the teachers are saying and some of them go really fast. It wasn't like that at my old school.

Luckily, we're in the last week of the first term and then we ⁶ _____ for two weeks. I'm really looking forward to the holidays this year.

3 Complete the sentences with the correct preposition.

1 A lot of people learn to drive _____ the age of eighteen.

2 I find it difficult to concentrate _____ two things at the same time.

3 My sister is thinking of applying _____ a place on a business course.

4 Dad is suffering _____ a really bad cold at the moment.

5 My brother isn't very good _____ German. He can hardly speak a word of it.

6 There was a big increase _____ the number of students passing the exam this year.

7 If I were you, I wouldn't worry _____ it too much.

8 There's no need to spend a lot of money _____ a new school bag.

9 I wasn't completely satisfied _____ my marks in the last couple of tests.

10 She spends a large amount _____ time looking at social media.

4 Complete the text with expressions from Exercise 3.

I'm going to ¹ _____ the position of teaching assistant at my local school. I'm pretty ² _____ working with people and also explaining things, so I think I could be useful for the school. I'd really like to help children with learning difficulties if possible. There has been a big ³ _____ the number of children who need extra help in lessons. Some of these students are very clever, but may ⁴ _____ problems which make it difficult to ⁵ _____ what the teacher is saying in class.

I ⁶ _____ hours _____ the application form for the job, so I hope I get it. I'm not too ⁷ _____ where I end up working. I'll just be ⁸ _____ the chance to help students learn.

Grammar 2 -ing form; infinitives

1 Choose the correct option to complete the sentences.

1 I think you can avoid *to pay / paying* fees for that course, but it depends on how much you earn.

2 It's worth *to get / getting* the right qualifications if you're interested in that kind of work.

3 I'm interested in *to become / becoming* a fitness instructor.

4 My brother loves *study / studying* geography. It's his favourite subject.

5 We must *to meet / meet* again soon.

6 I had a shower before *to go / going* out.

7 *Write / Writing* essays in a second language can be difficult.

8 Lin didn't feel like *to come / coming* out this evening.

9 I would really like *to have / having* no accent when I speak Russian.

10 It was too far *to walk / walking*, so we caught the bus instead.

11 It's important *revising / to revise* before an exam.

12 I went to the supermarket on my way home *to get / getting* something for my dinner.

2 Complete the sentences with the correct form of *remember* or *stop* and the -ing form or infinitive of these verbs.

go	have	lock	look	play	tell
text	visit				

1 Did you _____ the front door before leaving the house?

2 She _____ football when she hurt her knee.

3 After walking for more than five hours, we _____ a break.

4 I _____ to the seaside every year with my grandparents when I was younger.

5 I must _____ my friend with all the details of the school trip.

6 We didn't _____ our friends on the way home because we were late for the train.

7 What do you mean you didn't know about the party? I _____ you about it last week.

8 I was late, so I didn't have time to _____ in any of the shops.

3 Complete the conversation with the -ing form or infinitive of these verbs.

ask for	come	do	go	improve
learn	make	upload		

Elke: Hi Asha, do you remember [1] _____ that IT course with me a few years ago?

Asha: Yes, but I think I stopped [2] _____ to it after a couple of lessons because it was so difficult.

Elke: Well, there's another one with the same teacher – it's about [3] _____ websites.

Asha: But I don't even know how [4] _____ a photo!

Elke: Oh, come on. It's always fun [5] _____ something new. I'll send them an email [6] _____ more details.

Asha: OK, that'll be fine. My children often tell me I need [7] _____ my IT skills.

Elke: Great. Are you interested in [8] _____ with me to a judo course too?

Asha: No, definitely not! I think the IT course is enough for me.

4 Complete the text with the -ing form or infinitive of the verbs in brackets.

The Lumiar schools in São Paulo, Brazil were set up by businessman, Ricardo Semler. He has a company, Semco, which is very original. People may [1] _____ (go) to work when they want and employees are encouraged [2] _____ (take part) in important decisions about the company's future. His schools are similar because the students are used to [3] _____ (decide) what they want [4] _____ (study). If a student thinks a subject is worth [5] _____ (follow), then they are free [6] _____ (do) that. For example, if a student enjoys a certain type of music, they can [7] _____ (find out) all about its cultural origins.

[8] _____ (choose) your own lessons and subjects sounds fun, doesn't it? But the schools weren't set up just [9] _____ (give) students an enjoyable time. They must still [10] _____ (take) all the national Brazilian exams and the students normally do well in these. The schools simply avoid [11] _____ (teach) students basic facts like the capital city of a country because they know that students are able [12] _____ (get) this information from the internet in a couple of seconds.

⟳ Grammar references 11.2 and 11.3, p171 in Student's Book

Writing linking words and phrases (2); stating facts and opinions; writing a letter

1 Read the writing task. Then choose the correct options.

Write a letter (100–130 words) to a friend telling them about after-school clubs / activities at your school.

You should:
- describe the clubs / activities that are available
- suggest a new club you would like to start yourself.

1 You need to write a *story / letter*.
2 You need to talk about *your school / schools in general*.

2 Read a student's answer to the task in Exercise 1. Complete the sentences with words and phrases from the Learning Reminder.

Email Message

From: Shaheen
To: Kieran

Hi Shaheen

Hope you're well.

You asked me about my after-school activities.
1 _____ there isn't much to do in general, we do have a few good after-school clubs. We have a really good table tennis club and we can play every evening until 5 p.m.
2 _____ table tennis, we also have an art club where we can draw or paint. I go to that and it's fun. 3 _____ , it's only on once or twice a month.

I'd like to start an after-school computer game club, but I'm pretty sure the IT teacher doesn't want to make the computers available for this.
4 _____ this, it'd be really good to try to set up something like that.

Hope that helps. Keep in touch.

Kieran

3 Read the Exam Reminder. How can you show you are giving your own opinion?

_____

_____

Exam REMINDER

Stating facts and opinions

- Sometimes in the exam you need to state facts and then give your opinion on these.
- Present the facts in one paragraph and your opinions in a separate paragraph.
- Use expressions like *I believe, personally, in my opinion, to my mind,* etc. to show the reader that you are stating your own opinion.

4 Read and complete the Exam Task. Don't forget to use the Useful Language on page 135 of your Student's Book.

Exam TASK

Writing a letter

Write a letter (100–130 words) to a friend about the use of technology at your school. You should:
- describe what technology is being used
- explain how you think technology could be used more / better in the future.

Reading choosing the best option; multiple choice with one text

1 Read the Exam Reminder. Is the answer usually found in just one sentence of the text?

Brain games for dogs

1 As we all know, the brain is the body's control centre, managing everything from sneezing to swallowing. It is common for people to play 'brain games' to keep their minds active as they grow older. This often involves things like crosswords or number games like *sudoku*, but scientists in Vienna now think that dogs may get the same benefit as humans from doing certain activities.

Of course, it is impossible to get a dog to sit down
10 and do a crossword, but scientists have trained dogs to play games with a touchscreen. They even call it 'dog sudoku' and hope it can stop dogs from becoming bored and unhappy in their later life.

The Vienna research centre is called the Clever Dog Lab and has tested the touchscreen system on over 100 different types of dog. The dogs were prepared for the test in three parts. In the first part, the dogs learned to approach the screen but not touch the food that was put under it. In the second part, dogs learned
20 to match an image on the screen with a particular food. For example, when a coloured circle appeared on the screen, the dog would be allowed to eat some food which was put close to the circle. In the third part, no food was available, but the dogs were trained to press the circle with their nose.

When the dogs have done the training, the real tests can start. A small yellow circle appears and when the dog touches the circle with its nose, it receives some food. The circle moves to a new position and if the
30 dog correctly touches this, it receives another reward. In the final stage, dogs are shown a yellow and a red circle. If they choose the correct one, they also receive something nice. If the wrong one is chosen, the screen goes blank and the dog gets another chance.

Scientists were encouraged by the fact that older dogs were able to learn difficult new tasks. They also asked the dogs' owners to check if the brain games were having an effect on their pets and some owners were amazed to see the progress their dogs were
40 making. They also reported that the dogs were very excited before the weekly training sessions and only six of more than 100 dogs stopped coming to these. Although the tests will clearly need to be changed for humans, there does appear to be a strong link between keeping the brain active and general happiness.

2 Read and complete the Exam Task.

Exam TASK

Multiple choice with one text

For each question, choose the correct answer.

1 Scientists at the Vienna research centre
   A do tests on humans as well as dogs.
   B check people's brains while they're doing crosswords.
   C want dogs to stay happy when they get old.
   D are not sure how to study dogs' brain activity.

2 The training involved
   A one type of dog.
   B many different types of dog.
   C only older dogs.
   D 100 dogs.

3 In which part of the training was food given to the dogs?
   A Only in the first.
   B Only in the second.
   C In the first and second.
   D In all three parts.

4 In the test itself, the dog
   A can do the test again if it makes a mistake.
   B has to make a noise when it sees something.
   C does the whole test with one picture.
   D only gets food at the end of the test.

5 Some of the dog owners
   A said their dogs did not like the tests.
   B think older dogs cannot learn to do new things.
   C want similar tests for people.
   D made positive comments about the tests.

Vocabulary 1 parts of the body

1 Choose the correct options to complete the sentences.

1 I'll have to change my walking shoes. They really hurt my *toes / thumbs*.

2 The coffee I drank was too hot and I burned my *tongue / teeth*.

3 These trainers are really comfortable for your *shoulders / heels* when you do sport.

4 I picked up a hot plate and burned my *knee / finger*.

5 Your *neck / knee* is just below your head.

6 Your *ankle / elbow* is in the middle of your arm.

2 Which word does not belong in the group?

1	ankle	heel	neck	toe
2	shoulder	elbow	hand	knee
3	heel	thumb	finger	hand
4	teeth	lip	tongue	ankle
5	chin	thumb	forehead	mouth

3 Complete the sentences with these words.

beard	blink	bone	breathe	cough
eyebrows	laugh	left-handed		muscles
neck	sneeze	swallow		

1 If you walk a lot, then the _____ in your legs will probably hurt a bit the following day.

2 You _____ your food too quickly. You should take your time when eating.

3 Only ten per cent of the world's population is _____ .

4 Your _____ are mainly there to protect your eyes.

5 Our eyes _____ automatically when they get dry.

6 If you break a _____ , it can take weeks or months to get better, especially if it's in your leg.

7 Some things, like certain flowers and pepper, make me _____ a lot.

8 It takes a couple of weeks to grow a _____ .

9 It's so hot in here. I can hardly _____ .

10 The worst thing about this cold is that I _____ and sneeze every five minutes.

11 We use lots of muscles around the mouth to _____ , so watching a comedy is good for you.

12 I slept in the wrong position and now my _____ hurts today.

Grammar 1 adjectives; adverbs; *so* and *such*

1 Correct the order of the adjectives.

1 We ate Italian delicious cheap food in Rome.

_____

2 I bought a pair of big lovely woollen gloves.

_____

3 We stayed in a(n) German interesting old cabin.

_____

4 We saw a modern funny Greek comedy last night.

_____

2 Tick (✓) the correct sentences. Rewrite the ones that are incorrect.

1 I was absolutely amazing by their decision.

_____

2 The walk was really tiring.

_____

3 They weren't interesting in the details at all.

_____

4 The lesson was very bored for the students.

_____

5 I feel pretty tired after a few hours at the gym.

_____

6 We found the visit very interested.

_____

3 Tick (✓) the sentences where the adverbs are in the correct position. Correct the wrong ones.

1 My friends and I on Saturdays play volleyball.

_____

2 She's always laughing and smiling.

_____

3 Quickly he walked to the station.

_____

4 We were too tired to go out yesterday evening.

_____

5 The walk was tiring quite, but I enjoyed it.

_____

6 They often are at my local gym in the mornings.

_____

4 Complete the sentences with *so* or *such*.

1 He leaves _____ early each morning.
2 I've never heard _____ a noise before.
3 That film has _____ a good story.
4 I was _____ tired last night.
5 That was _____ an unkind thing to say.
6 Why did the film go on for _____ long?

Listening keeping calm; multiple choice with picture options

1 Read the Exam Reminder. Why do you need to be calm while you listen?

_____

2 🔊 12.1 ▶ Listen and complete the Exam Task.

Exam TASK

Multiple choice with picture options

For each question, choose the correct answer.

You will hear the recording twice.

1 What part of his body did Miguel hurt in the mountains?

 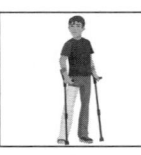 

A   B   C

2 What did the young child swallow?

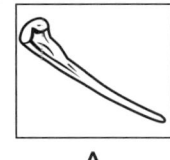  

A   B   C

3 When is Fabienne's operation?

A   B   C

4 What is Dipesh's temperature?

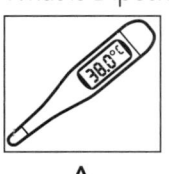 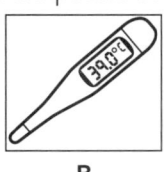 

A   B   C

5 How is Jonas going to get fit?

A   B   C

▶ Grammar references 12.1, 12.2 and 12.3, p171–172 in Student's Book

Vocabulary 2 injuries and illnesses

1 Choose the correct option to complete the sentences.

1 Did they have to *make / call* an ambulance?
2 Sami *broke / took* a bone in his hand.
3 The nurse *made / took* my temperature.
4 My shoulder *broke / felt* really sore.
5 She's recently *recovered from / made* a serious illness.
6 The doctor *wrote / called* a prescription for some medicine.

2 Complete the sentences with these words.

accident	appointment	better	cough
earache	finger	flu	operation	sore
shoulder			

1 Can you give me something for my _____ throat?
2 I've got terrible _____ and can't hear anything on that side.
3 I've been playing a lot of tennis recently and now have a really painful _____ .
4 I have a bad _____ , so none of my family got any sleep last night.
5 I always get _____ in winter.
6 I shut my hand in the door and now I can't write because my _____ is very painful.
7 My brother had a cycling _____ last month when a car hit him.
8 Yesterday I felt terrible, but today I feel much _____ .
9 It took me a long time to get back to normal after I had a(n) _____ on my back.
10 Can I make a(n) _____ to see the doctor?

3 Choose the correct option to complete the sentences.

1 I *did / went* on a diet after my holiday.
2 I try to *keep / go* fit, but I don't have much time.
3 My doctor says I should *catch / take* more exercise.
4 I often *take / catch* a cold on holiday.
5 It's difficult to *do / eat* a healthy diet when you have a lot of meals out in restaurants.
6 I *lost / made* a lot of weight after my operation.

4 Complete the text with these words.

call (x2)	flu	hospital	illness
prescription	sick	tablets	temperature
throat			

I had never had a serious [1] _____ until last week. I started feeling [2] _____ on Sunday evening. My mum took my [3] _____ and it was very high. I also had a really bad headache. She decided to [4] _____ the doctor and he came round about an hour later. He said I probably had [5] _____ and wrote a [6] _____ for some [7] _____ for my headache. By the next morning, I had a very sore [8] _____ and earache. My mum said I looked much worse than the day before, so she phoned the doctor again and he told us to [9] _____ an ambulance. I ended up staying in [10] _____ for a few days, but I'm back at home now and I feel a bit better.

5 Complete the text with these words.

accident	bone	diet	exercise	fit
healthy	ill	operations	painful	put on
recover from		weight		

My brother used to do a lot of [1] _____ and generally kept very [2] _____ . Recently though he's been looking a bit [3] _____ in my opinion. In fact, he's lost quite a lot of [4] _____ in the last couple of months. He had a bad [5] _____ last year when he broke a [6] _____ in his neck during a football match. He had two [7] _____ and it took a long time for him to [8] _____ them. His neck is still quite [9] _____ at times. Of course, he [10] _____ a lot of weight when he was at home and couldn't move around or do anything all day. That's when he decided to go on a special [11] _____ where he eats only certain types of fruit and vegetables. I told him just to eat [12] _____ food in general and to start doing some gentle exercise again. I hope he'll take my advice and start to feel better soon.

Grammar 2 comparison of adjectives and adverbs; thinking about the type of word; open cloze

1 Complete the sentences with the correct form of these adjectives.

| bad | cheerful | cold | fast | sad | tidy |

1 Why is your sister's room always _____ than yours? Yours is a complete mess!

2 That was the _____ film I've ever seen; I couldn't stop crying!

3 I heard this weekend is going to be _____ than the last one, so make sure you've got lots of warm clothes with you.

4 Heather runs _____ than Dana. I think she'll win the race.

5 Joey isn't as _____ as his sister. She's always laughing and smiling.

6 I sing _____ than all my friends. I can't sing a note!

2 Tick (✔) the sentences that are correct. Rewrite the incorrect sentences.

1 I think this film is best than her last one.

_____

2 That's the higher temperature I've ever had.

_____

3 The test wasn't as difficult like I'd expected.

_____

4 I can swim as fast as my brother now.

_____

5 I finished the test more early than my classmates.

_____

6 I'm definitely fitter now than when I started.

_____

3 Look at the first sentence. Complete the second sentence so that it has the same meaning. Use the words in brackets.

1 My mum works nine hours a day and my dad works nine hours too. (hard)

My mum works _____ my dad.

2 I start school at 8. My friends start at 8.30. (early)

My friends don't start school _____ me.

3 Both Franke and I speak good French. (well)

Franke speaks French _____ I do.

4 I haven't read a better book than this one. (the)

This is _____ I have ever read.

5 I can speak German more fluently than my dad. (fluently)

My dad _____ I do.

6 My cousin can run faster than anybody else. (fast)

Nobody _____ .

4 Read the Exam Reminder. How many words do contractions count as in the cloze task?

_____

5 Now complete the Exam Task.

Open cloze

For each question, write the correct answer.

Write one word for each gap.

Our hearts are essential to our survival. The heart is a kind of pump ¹ _____ works all day and night, often for up to 90 or 100 years.

When you wake ² _____ in the morning and feel relaxed, your heart normally beats around 60 times a minute. In situations of stress, anxiety and danger or simply if you drink a lot of coffee, this may increase ³ _____ 160 beats or more in a minute.

A woman's heart beats slightly faster ⁴ _____ a man's, even in normal situations. Some say that the brain is the ⁵ _____ important organ, but it can only survive for a few minutes ⁶ _____ the help of the heart.

↻ Grammar reference 12.4, p172 in Student's Book

Writing
using formal language; thinking about structure; writing an essay

Learning **REMINDER**

Using formal language

- In essays, you need to use more formal language.
- Avoid using contractions, e.g. *People don't do not exercise enough in general.*
- Try to put your ideas together with linking words. These will give you one longer sentence instead of two shorter ones, e.g. *You should breathe slowly for a few minutes. You should relax all your muscles at the same time.* → *While you breathe slowly for a few minutes, you should also relax all your muscles.*
- Use formal words and phrases instead of informal ones, e.g.

Informal	Formal
lots of doctors	many doctors
awesome	very good, excellent
the other week	recently
Their diet is terrible.	Their diet is not very good.
All my friends like …	Many teenagers like …

- Don't use exclamation marks (!).

1 Read the task. Think of some ideas for this essay and write them down. Then organise the ideas into an essay plan with different paragraphs.

> Everybody agrees that exercise is important to stay healthy, but doing this can be expensive. What can you do to keep fit and healthy without spending a lot on gyms or equipment?

2 Read a student's answer to the task in Exercise 1. Check if it has the same ideas as your plan. Then match the paragraphs in the essay with the points in the student's essay plan.

> **1** In this essay I'll try to show that it is possible to keep fit and healthy without spending too much money.
>
> **2** It's true that gyms and sports clubs can be very expensive, sometimes more than 50 euros a month!
>
> **3** Let's look at some solutions. Gyms and sports clubs are not the only way to stay fit. It's easy to find a free online workout and to use things like bottles of water to do exercises. Another way could be to play a team sport in the park or organise a sports tournament with a group of friends.
>
> **4** To sum up, I think it's awful that people have to spend so much to stay fit and healthy. However, people can easily organise enjoyable, free activities themselves.

Essay plan

A Summary of main ideas. _____

B Introduction: introduce the topic and explain the aim of the essay. _____

C Suggested solutions for keeping fit without spending too much. _____

D Problems: High cost of some fitness activities. _____

3 Read the student's answer in Exercise 2 again. The student has sometimes used language which is too informal for an essay. Underline the informal phrases and replace them with more formal phrases. Use the Learning Reminder to help you.

4 Read the Exam Reminder. How should you organise paragraphs?

Exam **REMINDER**

Thinking about structure

- It's really important to have a good plan when you write a formal essay.
- Highlight the main parts in the question that you need to include in your essay.
- Write down the points for each paragraph. Try to put these ideas together in a logical order. For example, if one paragraph is about problems, then the next one will be about solutions to these problems.
- Remember to give reasons for your ideas and examples where possible.
- You need to have a paragraph at the beginning to introduce your topic and one at the end as a conclusion.
- Go back and read your essay again for any grammar, spelling, word order or punctuation mistakes.

5 Read and complete the Exam Task. Don't forget to use the Useful Language on page 147 of your Student's Book.

Exam **TASK**

Writing an essay

How can young people make sure they eat a healthy diet?

Write an essay in about **100 words**.

Vocabulary

1 Read the descriptions. Write the names of the jobs from the box.

architect	athlete	camera operator	cook
firefighter	soldier		

1 I work in a small team. Some days are quiet and some are busy. When people call us, we often have to go quickly and save people. _____

2 My job is sometimes very dangerous. We do a lot of training and we sometimes work in other countries. _____

3 I spend most of my day outdoors, apart from in winter when I train in the gym. I often have a lot of people watching me during competitions. _____

4 My job is never relaxing. It's often very hot where I work and we get really busy at midday and again in the evening. _____

5 I love the design side of my job. I often start with a pencil and a piece of paper. A few years later, I can see the result of my work. _____

6 I have to be in the right place at the right time. You see my work on TV, but you never see me. _____

2 Choose the correct option to complete the sentences.

1 I'm not very *patient / shy* – I don't like waiting for people.
2 Stop being so *calm / lazy* and help me clean the house.
3 Don't be *nervous / jealous* about taking the test.
4 Jen is *unkind / miserable* because she lost her favourite necklace.

3 Choose the correct option to complete the sentences.

1 I think she's an excellent *candidate /qualification* for the job.
2 My dad lost his job last month and has been *full-time / unemployed* since then.
3 I've applied *on / for* a job as shop assistant.
4 I couldn't work all day, so I asked to work *part-time / full-time*.
5 She was brought *out / up* in South Africa.
6 My mum was a chemist, but now she's 65 and is happily *unemployed / retired*.

Grammar

4 Are the verbs in these sentences in the correct tense? Rewrite the incorrect sentences. Tick (✔) the correct sentences.

1 I'm not studying history at school this term. _____
2 Why do you look at those people over there? _____
3 My friend thinks of becoming a doctor. _____
4 He isn't remembering the name of the street. _____
5 I don't feel well, but I'm seeing a doctor later. _____

5 Complete the sentences with the correct form of the verbs in brackets.

1 Where _____ (you / go) on holiday this year?
2 I _____ (not / understand) that part of the film.
3 My course _____ (start) on September 1st.
4 My dad _____ (work) part-time now.

6 Tick (✔) the correct sentences. Rewrite the incorrect sentences.

1 Can I give you an advice? _____
2 Could I have a tea, please? _____
3 Sorry I can't help. I've got a work to do. _____
4 I need some informations from you. _____

7 Choose the correct option to complete the sentences.

1 How *much / many* time have we got?
2 I really need *a few / a little* advice about this.
3 Can you get *a few / a little* potatoes for dinner?
4 I got *a / some* great T-shirt for my birthday.
5 You need *a / some* special equipment.
6 Remember to get *a little / a kilo of* oranges.
7 I'd really like *drink / a drink* if we have time.
8 I think we need *some / a* bread for tomorrow.

Vocabulary

1 Complete the sentences with these words.

bitter	salty	sour	spicy	sweet

1 I love _____ things like cake and chocolate.
2 There's too much chilli and it's very _____ .
3 When I'm hungry, I prefer _____ snacks like crackers and crisps to chocolate.
4 I like really _____ fruit like lemons.
5 My mum loves _____ food and drink. She never puts sugar in her coffee or tea, for example.

2 Complete the sentences with these words.

bake	barbecue	boil	fry	grill	roast

1 The weather's good today. I can _____ some fish outside.
2 I'm going to _____ a chocolate cake later.
3 I need some oil to _____ this fish.
4 You need to _____ the pasta in water.
5 It's best to _____ the chicken in a hot oven for at least two hours.
6 Why don't you _____ those burgers instead of frying them so they're healthier?

3 Choose the correct option to complete the sentences.

1 I enjoy a biscuit with a big *mug / saucer* of tea.
2 I'll get a *knife / fork* to cut the vegetables.
3 There are some *plates / saucers* for the tea cups in the cupboard.
4 I think there's a *cup / jar* of jam in the fridge.
5 I start every day with a *jug / bowl* of cereal.
6 Bring a *bottle / box* of water with you.

4 Complete the sentences with these words.

bunch	glass	packet	slice	tin

1 Could I have a _____ of pizza, please?
2 We'll need a large _____ of beans as well.
3 Can you buy a _____ of grapes, please.
4 Yesterday, I ate a whole _____ of biscuits!
5 I'll have a _____ of milk, please.

Grammar

5 Choose the correct option to complete the sentences.

1 I couldn't come to the party last night because I *studied / was studying*.
2 Why *did you decide / were you deciding* to fry this and not grill it?
3 The teacher asked me a question, but I *didn't know / wasn't knowing* the answer.
4 What *did you do / were you doing* this time yesterday?
5 It started to rain while I *waited / was waiting* for the bus.
6 He *lived / was living* in Malaysia until 2018.

6 Complete the sentences with the correct form of the verbs in brackets.

1 I _____ (have) a shower when you _____ (call).
2 After the film we _____ (have) a snack and then _____ (go) home.
3 When I _____ (get) to the station, my friends _____ (wait) for me.
4 Where _____ (you/go) when I saw you this morning?
5 I _____ (not/listen) just now. What happened at the end of the story?
6 Marc _____ (sing) when Mr Wong _____ (walk) into the classroom.

7 Choose the correct form to complete the sentences.

1 *I'm not used / I don't get used* to getting up early.
2 It took me a long time *to be used / to get used* to the hot weather here.
3 *He's not used / He doesn't get used* to this kind of food.
4 *I'm being used / I'm getting used* to living here.
5 *Are you used / Do you get used* to them now?
6 Have you got used to *speak / speaking* French?

Vocabulary

1 Complete the sentences with these words.

cave	ocean	rainforest	stream	valley

1 We live in a very pretty _____ in the Alps with the mountains all around us.
2 A _____ is a warm and humid place with lots of plants, insects and birds.
3 We throw a lot of rubbish into the _____ and it kills a lot of fish.
4 We spent hours in an underground _____ . It was cold and wet.
5 There is a _____ at the end of my garden and I love the sound of the water.

2 Complete the sentences with these words and phrases.

climate change	fossil fuels	power station
renewable energy	solar power	

1 We need to do something to stop _____ .
2 _____ is a popular source of energy in hot countries.
3 Sources of _____ are the sun, the wind or water.
4 _____ such as oil are responsible for a lot of the world's pollution.
5 People aren't happy about the new _____ that is being built nearby.

3 Choose the correct option to complete the sentences.

1 They *collected / set up* rubbish from the beach.
2 Plastic is *breaking / destroying* our seas.
3 Oil from ships often *reaches / prevents* beaches.
4 We *removed / survived* over a hundred plastic bottles from the local river.

4 Complete the sentences with these prepositions.

from	in	into	onto	over

1 They turned an old factory _____ a cinema.
2 We ran _____ the station to the stadium.
3 There's a power station _____ the countryside.
4 We jumped _____ the train as it was leaving.
5 We waited for you for _____ an hour.

Grammar

5 Complete the sentences with the correct form of the verb in brackets.

1 I _____ (never / eat) this kind of food before.
2 She _____ (visit) over twenty countries in the last two months.
3 You're tired because you _____ (work) too much.
4 They _____ (study) Spanish for the past six weeks.
5 I think we _____ (see) this film before.

6 Complete the text by writing one word in each gap.

I [1] _____ been travelling a lot recently. I haven't [2] _____ to Asia yet, but I [3] _____ travelled to South America a number of times. I've [4] _____ to the Amazon rainforest in Brazil and I've [5] _____ telling all my friends about the cool things I saw. I [6] _____ been back in New York for a few days, but I'm already planning my next trip!

7 Look carefully at the use of articles. Correct them where necessary.

1 We need to do more against the climate change.
2 People don't want power station in the city.
3 The caves you can see are very old.
4 I'd like to be scientist one day.
5 We should spend more on the solar power.
6 I'd love to live by the coast.

8 Complete the sentences with a, an, the or –.

1 There's _____ really pretty stream near here.
2 We can help _____ planet by using _____ renewable energy.
3 I heard that _____ tourists leave a lot of _____ rubbish on _____ Mount Everest.
4 My sister's _____ doctor.
5 _____ Françoise lives near _____ River Seine in _____ Paris.
6 There are lots of _____ plants and _____ insects in _____ rainforest.
7 Did you bring _____ book we talked about _____ other day?

Vocabulary

1 Choose the correct option to complete the sentences.

1 I want to buy a new *leather / wool* scarf.

2 This is too *tight / smart*. Is there a larger size?

3 That's a really *loose / unusual* hat you've got. Did you make it?

4 This T-shirt is made of *glass / cotton*.

5 I need some *earrings / glasses* to go with the bracelet.

6 It's cold, so wear a *coat / tie* when you go out.

7 Those boots are so *antique / old-fashioned*.

8 My new *glass / leather* gloves are really soft.

9 Could you put my phone in your *pocket / ring*, please?

10 Shall we give Dad a *metal / silk* tie for his birthday?

2 Complete the conversation with these words.

cotton	fashionable	go with	label
loose	shop around	try on (x2)	

A: Hello. Can I help you?

B: Yes, please. I'm looking for a shirt to ¹ _____ this jacket.

A: Let's see. How about this one?

B: It feels lovely. Is it made of ² _____ ?

A: No, I don't think so. I'll just check the ³ _____ . Ah, here it is. It's 100% silk. It costs €80.

B: Wow, that's a lot for a shirt!

A. I know, but they're very ⁴ _____ this year. If you ⁵ _____ you'll find higher prices than this. Would you like to ⁶ _____ the medium size?

B: Yes, please.

A: Great. The changing room's over there.

...

A: So, how is it?

B: It's a bit ⁷ _____ . Can I ⁸ _____ the smaller size, please?

A: Yes, of course. I'll get it for you.

Grammar

3 Choose the correct option to complete the sentences.

1 I know someone *which / who* can help you.

2 I remember the place *when / where* we first met.

3 She's wearing a ring *who / which* belonged to her grandmother.

4 Which is the person *who / whose* earrings are lost?

5 My cousin, *who / where* lives in Spain, is coming to see me in the summer.

6 Spring is the time *who / when* I go out the most.

4 Complete the text with who, which, where, whose and when.

Everybody knows the shops ¹ _____ sell fashion on our high streets. I still use them ² _____ I need a new pair of jeans, for example. But my habits are changing and I now buy a lot of things on the internet. As a result, there are online stores ³ _____ know everything about me from my past visits. I have a friend ⁴ _____ daughter receives over fifty text messages a day from her favourite clothes shops. There are also some great sites ⁵ _____ you can create your own personal look with just a few clicks. I have another friend ⁶ _____ will only buy new clothes this way. But most people still want to try the clothes on, ⁷ _____ is why they continue to use traditional shops. But these shops should remember there are sites ⁸ _____ can compare the price of an article in hundreds of places in less than a second.

5 Read the text in Exercise 4 again. Which gaps can use that instead of the relative pronoun?

_____

6 Complete the sentences with before, until or as soon as.

1 Come and say goodbye _____ you leave.

2 I won't know my result _____ the teacher has marked everybody's tests.

3 You can have the newspaper _____ I've read this article.

4 Josh will be here _____ he's eaten.

5 I won't be able to relax _____ the exams are over.

6 I'll turn off all the lights _____ we go out.

Vocabulary

1 Choose the correct option to complete the sentences.

1 *Accommodation / Apartment block* is very expensive around here.

2 My *cottage / flat* is on the third floor.

3 I share my new apartment with two *neighbours / flatmates*.

4 It's nice living here, but the *rent / property* is so high.

5 We often eat out on the *balcony / ceiling* in summer.

6 Your book is on the top *ladder / shelf*.

7 Have you got *a kettle / an oven* to boil some water?

8 Just throw those things away in the *brush / bin*.

2 Complete the sentences with these words.

blanket	bookcase	cushion	duvet
pillow	sheet		

1 Most of my favourite novels are over there on the _____ .

2 I don't need lots of blankets to sleep well, just a good quality _____ .

3 I need a really soft _____ to sleep on otherwise my neck hurts the next day.

4 It's freezing outside. Let's put a thick wool _____ on the bed.

5 I have put a clean _____ on the bed.

6 If you need another _____ , just take one from the other sofa.

3 Complete the sentences with the correct form of these verbs.

do	make	move	take	tidy

1 I _____ my bed before going out this morning.

2 I don't want to _____ the washing up tonight.

3 Please _____ a seat.

4 We _____ away from this area a few years ago.

5 My parents were visiting, so I _____ my room.

6 I _____ the housework on Tuesday afternoons.

Grammar

4 Choose the correct option to complete the sentences.

1 I think *I'll go / I'm going to go* home now.

2 *I'll / I'm going to* visit my relatives in New York next month.

3 *Will you / Are you going to* help me with my homework?

4 I hope they *won't be / aren't going to be* late.

5 That building *will / is going to* fall down. It's in a really bad condition.

5 Match the beginnings of the sentences (1–6) with the endings (a–f).

1 When does ☐   a meeting Zara at 8.30 p.m.

2 I am ☐   b are we playing tennis this afternoon?

3 What time ☐   c going to pay for the tickets?

4 Hurry up! The bank ☐   d the film start?

5 How are we ☐   e to the island by boat.

6 We're going ☐   f closes in five minutes.

6 Complete the sentences with the correct form of *be going to*, *might* or *will* and the verbs in brackets.

1 Look at all those people at the entrance. It _____ (be) really full inside the stadium tonight.

2 Take your umbrella. You never know – it _____ (rain) later.

3 If you don't see me, just wait a few minutes. I _____ (be) a bit late because of the traffic.

4 I spoke to the teacher and we _____ (definitely / have) a test on Friday.

5 Be careful when you ski that fast. You _____ (crash) into somebody else.

6 I haven't seen the forecast, but I just hope it _____ (be) warm at the weekend.

7 Her work has been really good all year, so I'm sure she _____ (pass) the final exam.

8 You never know. You _____ (enjoy) the film after all.

Vocabulary

1 Complete the sentences with the correct form of *do*, *go* or *play*.

1 I _____ swimming every day.
2 My sister _____ aerobics every morning.
3 I'd like to _____ basketball later.
4 Jill _____ athletics for a year, but then stopped.
5 I haven't _____ judo for a long time.
6 They _____ running at the weekend.

2 Complete the sentences with these words.

indoor sports	net	pitch	racket	stick
track				

1 You need a special _____ to play hockey.
2 We play football on a local _____ . The grass is quite good in the summer.
3 I love running on a proper _____ .
4 I bought a new squash _____ and it's really light.
5 In winter, I prefer _____ so I don't get cold or wet.
6 You need to hit a ball over the _____ in both tennis and volleyball.

3 Choose the correct option to complete the sentences.

1 I'm going to *join / hit* the local skiing club.
2 Wear *gloves / a helmet* to protect your hands.
3 You need good *trainers / ice skates* to go running.
4 A *swimming costume / tracksuit* keeps you warm.
5 She *hit / scored* a great goal.
6 I'm not able to *sail / ride* a boat.
7 I *practised / did* my skills before the competition.
8 She *entered / joined* a judo competition.

4 Complete the sentences with the correct form of the word in brackets.

1 My personal _____ (free) is important to me.
2 I need to improve my _____ (fit).
3 My cousin wants to be a _____ (profession) basketball player.
4 He used to be a _____ (dive) instructor.
5 I'd like to swim _____ (compete), but I'm not fast enough yet.
6 My sister has an ice-skating _____ (compete) next week.

Grammar

5 Choose the correct option to complete the sentences.

1 I *call / 'll call* you if I have time.
2 If you use good equipment, you *ski / 'll ski* better.
3 If we *score / 'll score* in the next few minutes, we could win.
4 When you practise a sport with an instructor, *you get / 'll get* better at it.
5 I'm not sure, but if you leave now there *will / might* be less traffic.
6 f there's bad weather tomorrow, we *have to / will have to* train indoors.

6 Complete the second sentence so that it has the same meaning as the first.

1 There is a possibility it will rain tomorrow. In that case, we won't go.
   If it _____ .
2 Unless you practise more, you won't win.
   If you _____ .
3 If they don't improve their fitness, they won't get in the team.
   Unless they _____ .
4 It might be difficult to finish the race if you don't train harder.
   Unless you _____ .

7 Choose the correct option to complete the sentences.

1 If I *know / knew* how to speak German, I'd go and study there.
2 If we had a local athletics track, we *can / could* train more often.
3 I'll *score / I'd score* more goals in matches if I tried harder.
4 If we *play / played* on a good pitch, I think we'd get better results.
5 If I were you, *I'll start / I'd start* doing yoga.

8 Rewrite the sentences using the second conditional.

1 She doesn't have running shoes, so she doesn't go running.
   If she _____ .
2 I don't know the answer, so I can't help you.
   If I _____ .
3 We don't practise and we don't win games.
   If we _____ .

Vocabulary

1 Choose the correct option to complete the sentences.

1 I paid the correct *fare / journey* and got on the bus.

2 We're really close to the *border / currency*, so get all the passports ready.

3 Don't forget to take all your *fare / baggage* with you when you get off the plane.

4 Do we need a *reservation / currency* to eat there?

5 I need a tourist *border / visa* for the next three months.

6 We had a lot of problems and finally reached our *journey / destination* after midnight.

2 Complete the sentences with these words and phrases.

| boarding pass check out duty free |
| reception roundabout |

1 You can't get on the plane without a _____ .

2 You can pay for drinks and room service when you _____ of the hotel.

3 If you have questions, please ask the staff at _____ .

4 Leave the _____ at the second exit.

5 He bought some perfume at _____ before he got on the plane.

3 Complete the sentences with these words and phrases.

| by air campsite holiday home hostel |
| on board petrol station |

1 We stayed in a nice _____ and shared a room with six students from Bonn.

2 We're looking for a _____ on a Greek island as hotels are too expensive.

3 There are lots of things to do _____ the boat.

4 We stopped at a _____ just before the border and filled up the car.

5 The train is nice, but it's much quicker to travel long distances _____ .

6 Every _____ is full, so we'll need to put up the tent in the forest.

Grammar

4 Complete the questions with the correct question tag.

1 You travel a lot, _____ ?

2 We can't put our boarding passes on our phones, _____ ?

3 They're arriving soon, _____ ?

4 We must leave early, _____ ?

5 They followed us, _____ ?

5 Look at the situations and the questions. Write S (subject question) or O (object question).

1 David gave Sonia a present.

  a Who gave Sonia a present? _____

  b What did David give Sonia? _____

2 We booked a night in a hotel.

  a What did you book? _____

  b Who booked a night in a hotel? _____

3 I found a phone on the train.

  a What did you find on the train? _____

  b Who found a phone on the train? _____

6 Choose the correct option to complete the sentences.

1 They *had walked / had been walking* around the forest for hours before somebody found them.

2 Before she went to university, Rachel *had never visited / had never been visiting* a foreign country.

3 Carrie *had already reached / had already been reaching* the top when the others got there.

4 I *had known / had been knowing* my best friend for about six years before she moved away.

5 While I *had talked / had been talking* on the phone, I managed to burn the dinner.

6 I was surprised because when I got to the bus stop nobody *had arrived / had been arriving*.

7 Complete the sentences with the past perfect of the verbs in brackets.

1 When I got to the airport, I realised I _____ (leave) my passport at home.

2 She _____ (work) there for over two years before she decided to change her job.

3 He _____ (play) tennis for six months when he finally won his first match.

4 I _____ (know) about the surprise for weeks.

Vocabulary

1 Complete the sentences with these words.

| backpacking | graphic design | sailing |
| squash | using social media | |

1 I went _____ around Australia with a friend last year.
2 You play _____ indoors.
3 I like _____ to keep in touch with my friends.
4 I'd like to study _____ at college and then develop content for web pages.
5 You need to wear a life jacket when you go _____ .

2 Choose the correct option to complete the sentences.

1 I can't *stand / like* sculpture exhibitions.
2 I can't *do / write* music, but I love listening to it.
3 We *listened to / went to* an interesting podcast.
4 My friend *designs / watches* computer games.
5 You must wear *paintbrushes / trainers*.

3 Replace the phrase in italics with these words or phrases.

| come round | gave up | get together |
| hang out | join in | set up |

1 Some friends and I decided to *start* an environmental group at school. _____
2 I often *spend time* with my friends at the shopping centre. _____
3 Let's *meet* one evening for a pizza. _____
4 Would you like to *visit me at my house* later? _____
5 I tried to learn Chinese, but I *stopped* after a few lessons because it was so hard. _____
6 We're creating an after-school drama group. Would you like to *be part of it*? _____

4 Complete the sentences with these words.

| awesome | awful | challenging | frightening |

1 I can't stand this restaurant. The food is _____ .
2 The trek was very long and _____ .
3 That film's _____ . You must go and see it.
4 It was dark and we were lost in a strange place. It was a bit _____ .

Grammar

5 Complete the sentences with these words.

| can't | couldn't | might | must |
| ought to | shouldn't | was able to | |

1 I went to the concert, but I _____ see anything.
2 If you forgot his birthday, you _____ call and say sorry.
3 That _____ be Pete over there. He's the only person who wears hats like that.
4 It was difficult to get tickets, but in the end I _____ buy one online.
5 I _____ be late this evening. If I am, I'll send you a text.
6 You _____ still be thirsty. You've had three bottles of water already.
7 You _____ hang out with them if they're unkind to you.

6 Choose the correct option to complete the sentences.

1 Don't worry – you *don't have to / mustn't* have a visa to enter the country.
2 You *don't have to / mustn't* eat or drink in the classroom.
3 *Can / Need* I use your phone for a moment?
4 I really *must / need* finish this before I go out.
5 *Do we have to / Do we must* arrive early?
6 We *need to / can* leave as quickly as possible. I think they're going to close.

7 Tick the sentence (a or b) which matches the meaning of the first sentence.

1 It's necessary to have an international licence to drive in this country.
   a You don't need to have an international licence to drive in this country. _____
   b You must have an international licence to drive in this country. _____
2 We've got some bread in the kitchen.
   a You needn't buy more bread. _____
   b You must buy some more bread. _____
3 We can get her a present, but only if we really want to.
   a We mustn't buy her a present. _____
   b We don't have to buy her a present. _____
4 I need a phone. I'd like to use yours.
   a Could you lend me your phone? _____
   b You mustn't lend me your phone. _____

Vocabulary

1 Choose the correct option to complete the sentences.

1 We have to buy some new *server / hardware* for our computer system.

2 Mobile technology was a great *equipment / invention*.

3 This is a fast computer, but it needs the very latest *software / server* to run properly.

4 The *webcam / mouse* made it much easier to move around the computer screen.

5 With this *server / webcam* you can hold a meeting with up to 100 people.

6 Our *invention / server* is very slow, so your film might take a while to upload.

7 You can access the internet on your *smartphone / software*.

8 We need to buy some new *equipment / webcam*.

2 Complete the sentences with these words.

chat	connect	crashed	deleted
download	install	instructions	switch

1 The computer's still on. Can you _____ it off?

2 Can you help me _____ this program on my new PC? It's a bit complicated.

3 Why didn't you follow the _____ before you started using it?

4 I can't _____ to the internet this morning. Can anybody else?

5 I think you need to _____ this program from the internet.

6 With a good webcam you can see and _____ with friends all over the world.

7 Our computer system _____ last night and it took two hours to re-start it.

8 A virus _____ all my files.

3 Complete the sentences with the correct preposition.

1 I'm looking _____ a new webcam.

2 I bought a tablet instead _____ a laptop.

3 They carried _____ the work last week.

4 She's an expert _____ computer servers.

5 We succeeded _____ installing the program.

Grammar

4 Complete the sentences with the passive form of the verbs in brackets.

1 French _____ (speak) in many parts of Africa.

2 My new bike _____ (steal) last night.

3 The webcam _____ (can / use) with all kinds of computers.

4 All computers _____ (must / switch off) at the end of each working day.

5 Your computer _____ (should / check) for viruses every week.

5 Complete the sentences with *by* or *with*.

1 This experiment was carried out _____ a small laboratory.

2 This was painted _____ a very basic paintbrush.

3 The film is based on a book written _____ George Eliot in 1860.

4 The tablet should be cleaned _____ a special liquid.

6 Choose the correct option to complete the sentences.

1 When I got home I noticed that an upstairs window *had been broken / had broken*.

2 I couldn't use my car yesterday because *it was repaired / it was being repaired*.

3 The software *is being tested / was being tested* for a few hours yesterday afternoon.

4 The video of the school concert *had watched / has been watched* by thousands of people.

7 Complete the sentences with the passive form of the verbs in brackets.

1 When the parcel arrived, I saw that some of the pieces _____ (break) during delivery.

2 We can give you a car while yours _____ (repair).

3 A lot of houses _____ (damage) by terrible storms in the last few days.

4 Your smartphone _____ (check) right now.

Vocabulary

1 **Choose the correct option to complete the sentences.**

1 It's an interesting *drama / talent show* and the acting is wonderful.

2 I like *chat shows / thrillers* because you learn things about famous people.

3 I never watch *quiz shows / soap operas* because I don't know any of the answers.

4 There's a good *documentary / drama* on tonight. You can learn a lot from these programmes.

5 I never watch *horror / drama* as it's so scary.

6 My mum hasn't missed a single episode of that *documentary / soap opera*.

7 She's a big *celebrity / channel* in Brazil, but nobody knows her here.

8 I never watch the news because I can't stand the *series / presenters*.

2 **Complete the sentences with these prepositions.**

down	into	off	on	out	up

1 Can you turn the volume _____ a bit? It's too loud.

2 I was looking for something good to watch, but there was nothing on, so I turned the TV _____ and went out.

3 I tried to make a cake, but it turned _____ really badly.

4 My favourite song was playing on the radio, so I turned the volume _____ to the maximum.

5 I was tired, so I sat down, turned _____ the TV and watched my favourite soap opera.

6 My favourite clothes shop was turned _____ a fast food restaurant about a year ago.

3 **Choose the correct option to complete the sentences.**

1 I can't talk as I need to *end up / get on with* this project.

2 Be quick. You don't want to *run out of / be into* time.

3 Sadly, our holiday *is over / put off*.

4 What did you *run out of / put off* doing yesterday?

Grammar

4 **Rewrite the direct speech as reported speech.**

1 'We want to go home tomorrow,' they said.

They said _____ .

2 'Your parents are arriving soon,' she said

She said _____ .

3 'She hasn't called me,' I said.

I said _____ .

4 'You must study harder,' he said.

He said _____ .

5 'I saw them two weeks ago,' said Pat.

Pat said _____ .

6 'We couldn't see Kim at the concert last night,' they said.

They said _____ .

7 'I'll let you know tomorrow,' said Ilda.

Ilda said _____ .

5 **Complete the reported questions.**

1 'Did you go to the concert last weekend?' Susanna asked.

Susanna asked us _____ .

2 'Are you going to watch the documentary this evening?' Clare asked.

Clare asked me _____ .

3 'Have you finished your homework?' Miguel asked.

Miguel asked me _____ .

4 'Why didn't you watch the quiz show last night?' Natalie asked.

Natalie asked _____ .

5 'Are they going to call us tomorrow?' asked José.

José asked _____ .

6 'Can I come and visit you?' asked Jade.

Jade asked _____ .

6 **Rewrite the reported speech as direct speech.**

1 Mum asked me why I was leaving so early that morning.

_____ , asked Mum.

2 Astrid asked me if I had watched my favourite talent show recently.

_____ , asked Astrid.

3 Lucas asked us when he could come to our house.

_____ , asked Lucas.

Vocabulary

1 Complete the sentences with these words.

| degree | diploma | essay | examiner |
| failed | fees | grant | pupil | subject |

1 The _____ for this course are really high.
2 The _____ didn't like my pronunciation, so _____ me in the oral exam.
3 Physics is definitely my favourite _____ .
4 I have to write a long _____ about renewable energy.
5 You need a high school _____ if you want to study certain subjects at college or university.
6 I got a _____ to help pay for the course.
7 After three years at university, she got her _____ in computer science.
8 All his teachers say he's a good _____ .

2 Choose the correct option to complete the sentences.

1 Your parents would be happy if you *did / made* a bit more effort at school.
2 How will you *have / make* progress if you don't do any revision?
3 If you *take / break* the rules, you'll get in trouble.
4 We have exams now, but then we *make / break* up for a few weeks and I can visit my family.
5 It's difficult to *do / take* notes while you're listening in a foreign language.
6 I *did / made* a really silly mistake in the very last exercise. I'm so annoyed with myself.

3 Complete the sentences with the correct preposition.

1 We had a big increase _____ the number of students at our school.
2 She's worried _____ the test tomorrow.
3 I'm not very good _____ any kind of sport.
4 My mum applied _____ a job at the local hospital.
5 I'm suffering _____ a terrible cold.
6 She finds it hard to concentrate _____ her homework in the evenings.
7 Her teachers are satisfied _____ her progress.

Grammar

4 Complete the sentences using the causative.

1 Is somebody fixing your smartphone?
Are you _____ ?
2 My bike was repaired at the weekend.
I _____ .
3 A friend is going to check his homework.
He _____ .
4 I asked my cousin to take my photograph.
I _____ .
5 They'll get someone to deliver it to your home.
You _____ .
6 I need someone to sign my application form.
I _____ .
7 Did someone delete your message on the forum?
Did _____ .

5 Choose the correct option to complete the sentences.

1 I love *study / studying* languages.
2 I was really happy *to see / see* my friend again.
3 I really must *finish / to finish* painting the wall before I go out.
4 We stopped *to have / having* a break on our coach trip.
5 They remembered *to visit / visiting* that place many years before.
6 You're too young *to go / going* to university.
7 *Study / Studying* for a big exam can be difficult.
8 You'd better *tell / to tell* your parents about it.

6 Complete the sentences with the infinitive or *-ing* form of the verbs in brackets.

1 I went to the bank _____ (get) some money out.
2 Oh no! I didn't remember _____ (tell) Eduardo about the party.
3 I wasn't tall enough _____ (become) a professional volleyball player.
4 _____ (apply) for the right position is really important.
5 I must concentrate on _____ (do) my homework.
6 I was really glad _____ (hear) the good news.
7 She's interested in _____ (study) economics at college.

Vocabulary

1 Choose the correct option to complete the sentences.

1 The food was so hot that it burned my *tongue / elbow*.

2 There were no knives or forks, so we used our *lips / fingers* to eat.

3 I've hurt my *ankle / shoulder* and now I find it difficult to walk.

4 If you want to jump higher, you need to use your *knees / thumbs* much more.

5 I dropped a box on my foot and hurt my *toe / lip*.

6 These shoes are nice, but they're very tight on the *knee / heel*.

2 Complete the sentences with these words.

blink	breathe	eyebrows	left-handed
sneeze	swallow		

1 It can be difficult to _____ when you're high up in the mountains because the air is thin.

2 When I'm in a hurry, I _____ my food really quickly and then I feel ill.

3 My brother and I are very different. He's _____ , but I write with my right.

4 I _____ a lot when I don't wear my sunglasses.

5 Your _____ help keep things out of your eyes.

6 I _____ a lot in the spring when people start to cut the grass.

3 Complete the sentences with these words.

bone	call	ill	injury	recover from
sore	take			

1 I felt really _____ and they had to _____ an ambulance.

2 They told me I'd broken a small _____ in my foot and wouldn't be able to walk for a bit.

3 My leg felt really _____ after I fell off my skateboard.

4 The doctor says you have to _____ three tablets a day for at least a week.

5 It took him three weeks to _____ his illness.

6 The _____ wasn't too bad and I only needed a plaster.

Grammar

4 Write the adjectives in the correct order.

1 My friend has bought a _____ car. (new, big, black)

2 I'm reading a(n) _____ book. (French, interesting, old)

3 The pens are in a _____ box on my desk. (metal, green, small)

4 I got a _____ scarf for my birthday. (silk, orange, lovely)

5 Tick (✔) the two correct sentences. Correct the mistakes in the other sentences.

1 My legs were sore quite after the walk.
_____

2 I take always these tablets before breakfast.
_____

3 I haven't seen you for so a long time.
_____

4 We walked slowly to the park yesterday morning.
_____

5 I felt such ill at the weekend.
_____

6 I was amazing by their reaction.
_____

7 I thought the film was really boring.
_____

8 This room is not enough big for the party.
_____

6 Complete the second sentence so that it has the same meaning as the first. Use the words in bold.

1 I can swim faster than all my classmates. **(fast)**
None of my classmates _____ .

2 I haven't read a better book than this one. **(best)**
This is _____ .

3 You finish school at 4.30 p.m. I finish at 4 p.m. **(early)**
You don't finish school _____ .

7 Correct the mistakes in the sentences.

1 This is the longer illness I've ever had.
_____

2 This is the worse film I've ever seen.
_____

3 I'm tall as my cousin. _____

4 This holiday wasn't as good like last year's.
_____

NATIONAL GEOGRAPHIC LEARNING

National Geographic Learning,
a Cengage Company

New Close-up B1 Workbook, **3rd Edition**
Author: Alun Phillips

Publisher: Rachael Gibbon

Executive Editor: Siân Mavor

Senior Development Editor: Sarah Ratcliff

Director of Global Marketing: Ian Martin

Product Marketing Manager: Anders Bylund

Heads of Regional Marketing:

  Charlotte Ellis (Europe, Middle East and Africa)

  Irina Pereyra (Latin America)

Senior Content Project Manager: Nick Ventullo

Media Researcher: Jeffrey Millies

Art Director: Brenda Carmichael

Operations Support: Avi Mednick

Manufacturing Manager: Eyvett Davis

Manufacturing Buyer: Elaine Bevan

Composition: SPi Global

Workbook ISBN: 978-0-357-43403-1

National Geographic Learning
Cheriton House, North Way,
Andover, Hampshire, SP10 5BE
United Kingdom

Locate your local office at **international.cengage.com/region**

Visit National Geographic Learning online at **ELTNGL.com**
Visit our corporate website at **www.cengage.com**

Printed in Malaysia by Times Offset
Print Number: 12 Print Year: 2025